D1541356

PRAISE FOR RETHINK CREATIVITY

"We often think about creativity as applicable only to the "artist," but unlocking creativity has deep implications of what it means to be a better leader, entrepreneur, and investor. Rethink Creativity *will help push your boundaries to do just that."*

"Kang believes that anyone can be creative and Rethink Creativity *charts a path to make it happen. She does it with inspiration, intelligence, and energy that will transcend all genders, professions, and ages."*

"Rethink Creativity *is a must read for anyone looking to get out of their comfort zone to grow as a person and as a professional. No matter what your field of work is, being creative will improve how you understand yourself and others in order to be a better leader and team player. By sharing her personal story one can relate to the pressures of fitting into society's box. She will intellectually challenge you to accept yourself by providing exercises to foster your creativity - a key component of today's problem solving.*"

—LORENA VALENTE
Political Risk Consultant

"*In* Rethink Creativity, *Kang takes us on a journey to re-discover an important aspect of each of us becoming the best version of ourselves... and that aspect is our creative side. In person, Monica has a personality that lights up every room she enters. Her ability to make you feel like her best friend comes through effortlessly in her writing as she takes timeless principles and presents them in a way that is new, fresh, and easy to digest.*"

—SCOTT A. VOWELS
Supplier Diversity, Apple and Author,
Don't Be Afraid to Call the Baby Ugly

"*I'm an accountant by trade so there's not a lot that's creative about numbers! I've always viewed creativity as something you've got...or not. But what struck me about* Rethink Creativity *is the message that we all have to be intentional about creativity. I love the practicality of fostering creativity and am excited about the exploration Kang has set me on—to leave the comfort of familiarity to rethink my creativity.*"

—KELLY LEONARD
Author, *B.O.O.S.T.®*, TV Host & Executive Producer,
The Small Business Network

"Kang's book is a must-read primer for anyone seeking new ways to be creative. Complete with instantly actionable motivating tools and instruction, it will give you the edge you need to reignite passion and innovation in your work and life."

—LINDSAY YOUNG
Attorney

"Rethink Creativity is the book that we all need to read, at this time and in this moment. It provides a step-to-step guide on how to unlock your creativity, to empower your team, to be happier, to be more creative, and to be more human. In the corporate world and in your own life, the words of wisdom, the exercises, and the gems of deep, insightful knowledge will change your life and your perspective. Kang's story is a testament to the human capacity to be introspective, be proactive, be courageous, and march forward into one's bliss. The honesty and vulnerability that underpins this work will unlock things that you forgot or were unaware of."

—DR. TYRONE GRANDISON
Founder, The Data-Driven Institute

"If you are in a creative rut then Rethink Creativity *and Kang's philosophy on how to break through the conforming and siloed ways of problem solving is a must read."*

—G. NAGESH RAO
Eisenhower Fellow and AAAS-Lemelson
Invention Ambassador Advisory Board Member

"I'm taking action to add creative time to each and every day - including a walk at lunch with my camera. This small adjustment in my daily routine leaves me inspired and refreshed. I come back from my lunchtime photo safaris ready to tackle even more challenges with a fresh perspective. This simple exercise has helped me find the creativity I've always had and because I've become even truer to myself, it's having an impact on my management style. I find that I'm more empathetic with my team. I mix up how we run things to help the team out of ruts. I look for opportunities to praise small increments of creativity rather than just the big wins, when we face a challenge. I set boundaries allowing the team to truly think outside of our usual box. And, I help the team celebrate failures. All of this has made us a stronger, more resilient and definitely more creative team."

—JESSICA COLLISON
Director of Research for a Global Trade Association

—————————————

"Kang gives us new tips until we arrive at the same destination: the spark of creativity, freedom from fears, assumptions and societal expectations, and the courage to be human-being and not "human-doing," a better team player and a better leader."

—DR. KHULOUD ODEH
CIO, Urban Institute

—————————————

"Kang writes an amazing how-to manual that doesn't feel prescriptive. Instead, I felt inspired to embrace my own journey and individuality as I approached her experiences and learnings. It was great connecting to her personal story—hearing Kang describe her path into this work as a journey of discovery for her. Within the first few pages, I could quickly see what the value of a book like this could be for me in my own journey and how I would use this as a resource to hold myself accountable for not repeating cycles of stress and unhappiness in my professional or personal life. Creativity isn't a novelty concept—it's a key part of a healthy approach to life, and Kang shows us ways we can incorporate it consistently in our lives."

—COREY PONDER
Privacy Program Manager, Facebook

"While there are many books on creativity, Kang takes a fresh approach by inviting readers to engage with their creative potential, instead of just reading about it."

—DR. STEVE RALPH
Faculty, Pepperdine University Graziadio Business School

"Rethink Creativity *is essential reading for anyone looking to reboot their creative engines."*

—DARON K. ROBERTS, J.D.
Founding Director, Center for Sports
Leadership & Innovation, The University of Texas

R_ETHINK CR^EATIVITY

How to INNOVATE, INSPIRE, and THRIVE at WORK

Monica H. Kang

Founder & CEO of InnovatorsBox®

PUBLISH
YOUR
PURPOSE
PRESS™

For permission requests, write to the publisher, addressed "Attention: Permissions Coordinator," at the address below.
Publish Your Purpose Press
141 Weston Street, #155
Hartford, CT, 06141

The opinions expressed by the Author are not necessarily those held by Publish Your Purpose Press.

Ordering Information: Quantity sales and special discounts are available on quantity purchases by corporations, associations, and others. For details, contact the publisher at the address above.

Edited by: Heather B. Habelka
Cover design by: Monica Escobar Beasley
Illustrations by: Monica H. Kang
Interior book design by Designs Done Now

Printed in the United States of America.
ISBN: 978-1-946384-30-0 (paperback)
ISBN: 978-1-946384-40-9 (hardcover)
ISBN: 978-1-946384-31-7 (ebook)

Library of Congress Control Number: 2018946994
First edition, September 2018.

Publish Your Purpose Press works with authors,
and aspiring authors, who have a story to tell and
a brand to build. Do you have a book idea you
would like us to consider publishing? Please visit
PublishYourPurposePress.com for more information.

TABLE OF CONTENTS

19   **Foreword**

23   **The Beginning**

31   **Before You Start**

35   **1 There Is No One Perfect Formula**

45   **2 Who You Associate with and What You Observe Matters**

55   **3 The Best Things Don't Happen Overnight**

65   **4 Constraints—Your New Best Friend**

79   **5 The Power of Knowing Your True Self**

89   **6 Your Best Tools Are Rooted in Curiosity**

103   **7 A Thousand Shades of Failure**

115   **Conclusion**

123   **Author's Thoughts**

127   **Additional Resources**

131   **Key Tools**

137   **About the Author**

139   **About InnovatorsBox®**

143   **Footnotes**

To those who thought creativity was a foreign concept:

Welcome to the friend you never knew you had.

"Imagination is more important than knowledge."

—ALBERT EINSTEIN
Physicist, Scientist

FOREWORD:
Surround Yourself with Creative Believers

BY ADAM SMILEY POSWOLSKY

I can break my life into two periods of time: the time before I thought of myself as a creative person, and the time after I stepped into my creative power. For me, that line in the sand was drawn six years ago, when I was 28 years-old. Before 2012, I didn't think of myself as creative. I was stuck in an unfulfilling 9-to-5 job. My work was boring and monotonous. I felt like I was living someone else's life. I had panic attacks before falling asleep. I had trouble waking up in the morning. When my alarm clock would go off every morning at 6:30am to NPR, I'd want to throw my alarm clock out the window.

Everything changed for me in February 2012, when I attended the StartingBloc Institute for Social Innovation in Los Angeles, California. All my life, I enjoyed writing, but at StartingBloc, I met 100 other creative entrepreneurs and leaders who encouraged me to follow my dreams of actually being a writer. Through this community, I met people like Debbie Sterling. Debbie was starting GoldieBlox, a toy company that teaches young girls to become engineers. I met people like Evan Walden. Evan was launching ReWork, a company that helps people find meaningful work. And I met people like Monica Kang, who built InnovatorsBox®, a firm that helps people and their organizations grow their creative mindsets.

People like Debbie, Evan, and Monica believed in me and believed in my creative power. They held me accountable to quitting my unfulfilling job, moving across the country to San Francisco, starting a blog, and becoming a published author.

I learned two important lessons in my creative journey that *Rethink Creativity* will help you explore in greater depth. First, creativity is universal. Everyone can be creative. Everyone is creative. The only barrier between you and your creative power is yourself. If you want to be a writer, write. If you want to be a speaker, start speaking. If you want to become a designer, cool, you are already a designer. If you want to build a business, do it. Today. Not tomorrow. The point is, don't ask for permission. The only person who can give you permission to start making things is yourself.

The second and even more important lesson—and the reason I'm friends with Monica Kang—is that you can't be creative alone. If you want to live a life that matters, surround yourself with people that believe in the beauty of your creative dreams. No book is created by one person. No business is built without a team. No community is developed without the contributions of many. Before 2012, I was walking alone. After 2012, I had people like Debbie, Evan, and Monica to hold me accountable.

Surrounding yourself with creative believers will help you finish the book you've been wanting to write, the website you've been meaning to build, and prototype the product you've been dreaming about forever. Surrounding yourself with believers will help you find the right partner, the right friends, and the right people to work with. Surrounding yourself with believers will help your team and your organization succeed. Surrounding yourself with believers will help you find joy, inside and outside of your work.

The lessons in this book might seem simple at first, but they have changed my life. In the past six years, stepping into my creative power has helped me write three books (soon to be four!), book over 200 speaking engagements, build a profitable business working for myself, and travel all around the world meeting communities of purpose-driven millennials. More importantly, I love my life and I no longer want to throw my alarm clock out the window every morning.

Monica is one of the most creative people I know. Spending time with her is like stepping off an airplane and taking a breath of fresh air. I always leave our meetings with fifteen new ideas about how to approach something I'm struggling with. I remember attending her creativity workshop several years ago, and within twenty minutes, I was drawing with colored pencils and playing with playdough for the first time since elementary school.

The creative journey is never ending and never easy, but certainly is a lot more fun with this book, so thank you, Monica. I wish I had this book when I was beginning my journey as a writer six (well actually, thirty-five!) years ago. It would have reminded me not to be afraid of making mistakes. It would have reminded me to liberate myself from my own expectations, and the expectations of my parents, friends, and society. It would have given me the permission slip I needed to be free and simply listen to the words that were flowing out of my heart. Chances are, if you're reading this book, a creative breakthrough is calling you. I can't wait to see what you create and what we end up creating together.

—ADAM SMILEY POSWOLSKY
Author of The *Quarter-Life Breakthrough*
and *The Breakthrough Speaker*
San Francisco, California

THE BEGINNING

"Most people overestimate what they can do in one year and underestimate what they can do in ten years."

—BILL GATES
Entrepreneur, Philanthropist, Innovator

Do you ever wake up wishing today could somehow be better...or different?

Or wonder how you've ended up here?

Or thought that somewhere along the way you'd taken a wrong turn?

I remember asking myself these questions one morning during my commute. After rubbing my red, bleary eyes and releasing the heavy sighs that weighed down my body, I was startled by the reflection I saw in the bus window.

The woman staring back at me that morning on the bus looked unhappy, scared, and defeated. I didn't recognize her. How could I feel so stuck in a job I loved?

You see, growing up I had a clear vision of what I wanted to do. From jobs to education to love to life experiences, I was determined to build the career and life that I thought would be fruitful. I learned to be fearless and diligent in everything I pursued.

I'd lived in three continents, worked in five industries, and found work I was passionate about. I worked so hard to get here—I'd built a career in international affairs that I found fulfilling, traveled around the world, surrounded myself with good friends, and lived in a city I loved. From Geneva, Vienna, Seoul, Beijing to DC, there was not a dull moment as each experience brought new adventures. Yet there I sat on the bus that morning, unable to remember the last time I was excited to start my day. I used to feel energized when I woke up in the morning. I used to love my commute to work. And the fact that I couldn't remember when this shift happened terrified me. I was starting to feel depressed.

Dreaming big was not the problem. However, no one warned me that being ambitious also meant that I could get good at imagining worst-case scenarios and experiencing disappointment. The more I wanted to accomplish, the more I feared failing. I did not want to be the only one who did not get the government job all my friends got. I did not want to be the one who did not get that promotion I worked so hard for. I did not want to feel left out, so I forced myself to fit into the office culture, the job requirement, the job title, the good friend expectation, and the industry. But the more I tried to fit in, the more I came to realize I was letting go of who I was as a person. I let my fear drive me. And that made me realize enough was enough. It was time to shake up the status quo.

At first, I started with small changes, such as my commuting method or break in the office. Instead of taking the 25-minute bus ride I took a 45-minute walk. Instead of going to my regular Starbucks spot I started taking 30-minute walks around the neighborhood or going to a coffee shop three blocks farther away. I started listening to music that I usually do not listen to and attending events where I barely knew anyone. In the beginning I barely noticed how these changes were making a difference, let alone making me more creative. But over time I found myself getting more curious and more energized.

One day I even went to the art supply store to buy a set of color pencils and a sketchbook. I went to the Georgetown waterfront to sit and sketch the ducks and the sunset. I was struck by how everyone assumed I was an artist. And by how many assumptions we make in our routine without wondering why, without pressing for a deeper answer. Why do we assume being stuck in a job we love is normal? Why do we think it is weird to see someone sketching in the streets unless they are an artist?

The more I learned to let go of society's expectations and let myself define who I could become, I found myself not only being liberated, but also growing exponentially. It was in these moments that I reconnected with my creativity, and set myself on a course to create a movement. I started to reflect on how my life would be different if I could bring 100% of myself, my true self, to everything I did—including my work in nuclear security. (Yes, nuclear security!) I realized that by being more creative and giving myself more time to be creative, I was transforming the way I live.

But what
is creativity?

Today the term *creativity* has become an overused buzzword—one that is part of the corporate jargon and one that has been held exclusively for use by artists, musicians, or poets.

But these definitions are not true. Creativity is a way of living. And incorporating creativity into our work, regardless of our title or industry, gives us limitless potential.

I know, from firsthand experience, that when you reconnect with your creativity, you are able to build a creative mindset. This means you learn not only how to ideate and problem-solve, you also learn how to be more collaborative, understanding, open-minded, and patient.

This is why leaders who are creative are better problem solvers, communicators, and innovators. When you live more creatively you recognize that challenges are not obstacles but opportunities to grow. When you think more creatively you recognize different opinions are resources to think of new ways to solve problems.

Most importantly, you start to recognize that being creative is, at its core, what it means to be human.

It's no coincidence that you "feel alive" or "lose track of time" when you are immersed in a creative activity— from working in an Excel spreadsheet to painting a room in your home to preparing a meal. We were all naturally creative when we were children. We didn't think about it, we just created. It was effortless. Unfortunately, somewhere along the way, we received the messages that growing up meant growing out of creativity.

This is why we feel limited, stuck, and trapped when creativity is absent from our lives.

But when you unlock your creativity, you can share your gifts with the world—just like what happened to me that day on the bus.

Recognizing that I was in control of my creative strength and growth, I proactively took the step to make time to be creative, to try new things, and to learn from them. As a result of this conscious change, my performance in the office skyrocketed, I improved relationships with clients, got more done with less time, and got a promotion. Most importantly, I started to enjoy going to work and loving the job that I had struggled in.

And after many coffee meetings with friends who asked how I made this transition, I realized I could help more people—beyond consuming copious amounts of caffeine!

This is why I started my creative education company InnovatorsBox®, and this is why I set out to write this book.

Unfortunately, what I experienced is common. According to Gallup's 2016 research, about 87% of the world's population feels stuck at work due to a lack of creativity. And about 65% of Americans in corporations feel stressed daily.

It seems that we've come to expect that living a stressful, frustrating life that feels limited is "normal." So we settle. If we are simply doing things for the sake of it then we are *human-doing* not *human-being.*

Think about this:

* What if more people woke up feeling limitless instead of stuck?

* What if more people went to work feeling happy, creative, and confident—regardless of their job, industry, or age?

* What if schools prepared students to strive through challenges instead of focusing on the limitations? And taught them how to own their unique talents instead of comparing themselves to others?

I learned, through my own journey, that building a creative mindset is not only possible—it is critical to finding success in the workplace and joy in our personal lives.

I want you to know that you do not have to feel stuck, stressed, or limited. I want you to know that you are good enough and that you can trust your unique gifts. There is a way out of what is often called as a "funk"— and for me that showed up as depression.[1] While the path to restoring your creative mindset is not always easy, it will be enriching and exciting if you explore it with an open mind.

My hope is that by the end of this book you will rethink your own creativity, examine how you define yourself as a creative, and know how to bring your unique creativity into your workplace.

I am certain that as a workforce, we can make better decisions, develop better leaders, and create better organizations by learning how to harness the power of a creative mindset.

I believe this is possible because it is true.

Do you believe in your limitless potential?

I do.

With love,

Monica

It's no coincidence that you "feel alive" or "lose track of time"

when you are immersed in a creative activity.

BEFORE YOU START

Before we start, I want to briefly explain my approach to the creative mindset by outlining what I will (and won't) cover in this book.

There is nothing less fun than going on a journey with the wrong expectations. You don't want to end up in the mountains if you were expecting a day at the beach. Take a few minutes now to set your intentions for this journey: why did you pick this book, what are you hoping to get out of it, where do you want to go, and how do you intend to get there?

Trust that your intentions will guide you.

This book will help you appreciate how to:

* Look at creativity as more than a simple tool— because it isn't.

✳ See challenges as beautiful opportunities to grow and shine.

✳ Release limitations, regardless of your job title or industry.

However, here's what **not** to expect from this book:

Strategies on how to ideate products. There are enough books about that topic. And to be honest, we don't need more people in the workplace who follow a formulated approach to everything. We are looking to empower the workforce so they are ready to tackle complex problems in a whole new way by learning how to cultivate and embrace a creative mindset that is unique to them.

Immediate results. Just like you should not expect to lose weight after one day at the gym, your most pronounced changes will emerge over time and with ongoing effort. Continue to work hard, reflect, and flex your creative muscles and your best results will emerge—when you have built a creative mindset and successfully incorporated it into your daily routine.

To best witness the impact of the work you're going to do, don't forget to document every step along the way. Take some time to jot down your thoughts on what you really think about creativity, your creative thinking, and how you feel about your career—before and after you've read this book. This is your journey. The more space you give yourself to be honest and reflective, the more you will get out of it.

Trust that your INTENTIONS will guide you.

1
THERE IS NO ONE PERFECT FORMULA

"To define is to limit."
—OSCAR WILDE
Author, Playwright, Poet

I **don't have to be a magician to know** that there is no one else who is wearing what you are wearing in this exact moment. And no matter where you are, it is highly unlikely that you will pass by, or be in the same room with someone who is wearing exactly the same pair of glasses, shoes, shirt, or bag as you are—even if you wear a uniform for work or for school! To take this theory a step further, I'm also pretty sure that your preferences for spicy food, horror movies, and even sex are probably not the same either.

This is normal.

Because as beings, humans have diverse personalities,

preferences, experiences, communication styles, and biases. Just like our unique fingerprints, we are all different—from the way we live, enjoy, express, and excel. This is why when a group travels together, everyone will leave with different experiences, insights, and impressions even if they all took the exact same trip. We understand these kinds of differences.

So why do we expect creativity to mean the same for all of us?

The number one mistake we make in understanding creativity is associating it solely with art. Yes, art is creative but so are a lot of other things. Truth be told, we are probably expressing different forms of creativity every single day, but it's just that many of us are not giving it proper credit or association. To truly understand how we are all creative, you have to first see how diverse our creative expressions are. Some may feel more creative when they perform. Others may feel at their creative best when they are solving a complex mathematical formula or thinking of a unique way to solve a business problem. The manifestations of our creativity are as unique as our personalities.

It's critical for you to first honor how different everyone is and to understand your unique creative strengths and expressions. What act of creation makes you feel the most alive and energized? It may be writing, analyzing, speaking, or drawing. For others, it may be singing, building, designing, or performing. Whatever it is, it's the kind of activity that makes you lose track of time, one that you want to master, and that makes you the happiest person. But you have to do the work to understand what that is for you, or have the courage to acknowledge it.

For instance, how do you expect to know what your favorite taco in town is without first trying ones from different restaurants? When it comes to your creative preferences, you'll also need to try different things and be willing to identify what makes you thrive.

Feeling a bit lost? Let me break it down for you. Once you understand that everyone is wired differently when it comes to creativity, you'll also realize that everyone's creative process is different from how they are inspired (input) to what they create (output) to how they communicate the form of creation (expression).

This is why not all writers are inspired by, or use the same method, to write. It's also why two people who are both inspired by music may express their creativity by cooking or by working in Excel. While it may take some time to understand what input, output, and form of expression inspires you to be the most creative and energized version of yourself, you will come to understand what situations allow you to have the best creative flow. And once you understand what makes you the happiest, it becomes a lot easier for you to seek it out, or identify it in your daily work. Going back to the food example: It is a lot harder to enjoy a taco when you don't know which restaurant or food truck to visit!

The more you know about yourself, the easier the process of reconnecting with your creativity, and developing a creative mindset, will be.

REFLECT

Take out your notebook and be absolutely honest with yourself as you answer these questions. The more mental clarity you have, the more you will understand what truly makes you feel more creative. If it has been a while since you asked these questions, it's okay to come back to this as you walk through your reflection.

✴ When was the last time I felt creative? What was I doing? Why was I feeling creative?

✴ What do I love creating? Why?

While there isn't a single, perfect formula for creativity, we do get the benefit of such a rich diversity of creative results and forms of expression.

Imagine how boring the culinary world would be if everyone only cooked one style of tacos?

APPLY

Has it been a while since you practiced creativity? No fear. The key is to start spending five minutes every day to be creative. How? By doing something different.

Find ways to insert creativity into your day-to-day routine by trying something new. Attend events where you can learn a new perspective. Join a community where you know you may be a minority. Listen to new music from a band you never heard of. Take a new route to work. Travel to a new city where you don't speak the language. Order a different pasta for dinner. All of these ideas can help you stay alert to different resources, be curious, and remember that there is always something to learn. Consistency, not intensity, is key as you work to activate your creative thinking muscles.

It's also important to track and reflect on what you are learning from your experiences.

When we reflect and measure our progress we are able to better understand what works, what does not, and why. It also helps us stay motivated and keep things in perspective. And the more you explore, the higher the chance you'll find your best creative space.

As a leader, I challenge you to also apply this information to the team you manage. No matter what kind of company you have, your people matter. The people you hire, bring together, and work with directly contribute to what you develop and sell and how you grow your business. No matter how good an idea is, if you have a team that is not working together or is not confident, then your company will be short lived. On the other hand, when you have a collaborative team with diverse talent, they thrive both professionally and personally. Most organizations strive to create that space for their people. Yet many fail miserably. I believe one of the reasons is because they fail to provide a space for their people to grow, explore, and be creative. What if there is a way to better understand how to be creative, how to build a creative culture, and foster that innovation in a company by investing in your people and their mindset?

Just like everyone will choose different ways to develop their individual creativity, everyone will need different ways to develop their creativity in the office. Think environment, communication style, and prompts as you help employees embrace their creativity. One communication style, or way of problem-solving, won't resonate with every team member!

Take a moment to be honest with yourself and reflect on how you can better encourage your team members to bring their full selves to work. Perhaps you are insisting that others follow your approach to creativity? Just because you feel comfortable with your process does not mean the rest of your team members will. If you want to truly nourish your team's creativity and diverse interests, you have to be mindful of how you communicate, measure, and reward creativity and innovation.

The good news is that this process does not have to be hard or time consuming.

Here is a three-step approach to help you get started:

First, start by getting to know your team members and asking them to share more about their preferences. For instance, in communication, what works best for them, what doesn't, why, and what would they like to learn more of? If they answer "It doesn't matter," or "I don't know," encourage them to take the time to self-reflect in order to help them get specific.

Second, set a ground rule and the expectation that the team can agree on. Are there ways team members can highlight if something is not working? What is the cue to ensure everyone's voice is heard equally in a meeting? Whether you set a physical reminder using tools such as a talking stick, the key is that all team members contribute to setting the ground rules, agree to the details, and hold each other accountable.

Last, provide a clear and consistent feedback loop when things are done well or when the team falls short. If you said you wanted a team that encourages risk, visibly compliment the team member who took risks, whether that product was a success or not. If you said you wanted the team to be more open-minded, consistently find a way to acknowledge and compliment those actions. When such feedback is consistent, team members will have an easier understanding of how to bring creativity to the office, even if they approach or communicate it differently than you.

When your team members know the workplace is open to the expression of new ideas, where they will not be judged or held responsible if they fail, they are more likely to speak up and try executing the new ideas. Building that genuine trust to encourage creativity requires patience and an open mind. But you shouldn't expect to understand everyone's unique creative insights overnight, or expect them to completely change the way they work. However, constant communication, consistent action, and patience will encourage your team members to gradually open up. It may even inspire others to find their own creativity.

RECAP

Everyone is creative. To know your creative strengths, you've got to better understand what input, output, and expression inspires you to be the most creative version of yourself.

Inside the InnovatorsBox®

ReImagine is our motivation and inspiration series. Want to be more creative, but not sure how? No worries. Building a creative mindset is not an overnight transformation. It's a long and messy process, but it starts with taking small daily steps. You can have your dose of creative reminder either through the ReImagine notebooks or ReImagine cards, which is a deck of cards with 60 prompts to break your ordinary routine with creativity. Or use both to stay extra inspired.

5 Minutes of Daily Creativity Consistency is key. Making time to do something different every day for five minutes can be a powerful way to practice thinking differently and pausing. Choose a time of day in the office when you can give yourself five minutes of doing something different.

NOTES

2
WHO YOU ASSOCIATE WITH AND WHAT YOU OBSERVE MATTERS

"Movies can and do have tremendous influence in shaping young lives in the realm of entertainment towards the ideals and objectives of normal adulthood."

—WALT DISNEY
Entrepreneur, Animator

Parents care very much about where their children go to school. This is because we form our opinions based on our experiences. Teachers and classmates will influence who their children meet, what they learn, what they hear, what they believe, and what they think is possible for their future. School is where we form our initial thoughts, perspectives, and even definitions of friendship and love. This is why Jim Rohn famously said, "We are the average of the five people we spend most time with." It makes sense. The people you surround yourself with will significantly influence who you become and what you think of the world.

If we understand this to be true, then why do we have such a difficult time understanding the importance of being open-minded and welcoming diverse experiences and thoughts in the workplace? Creativity is the act of thinking differently. But what we forget to talk about is the subjectivity of thinking differently.

If I asked someone who has never experienced any form of poverty to think of different ways to live homeless in the streets, they would be challenged to think creatively compared to someone who has experienced it for themselves. If I asked someone who has never left their home how to travel the world on a tight budget, their answer would probably be quite different from someone who has a passport full of stamps. Our experiences, relationships, and associations directly reflect what we think is different or familiar, and therefore, influence what we think is creative or not.

So if we accumulate more experiences and increase our awareness, we will most likely be able to connect the dots in unique and creative ways. When we surround ourselves with a diverse group of friends, we can not only form a deeper appreciation and understanding of diversity of thoughts and complex opinions, but we can also find more creative approaches to problem-solving and understanding than someone who may only have one group of friends. Their cognitive horizons tend to be relatively narrower.

This is why the second important way to practice being more creative is to diversify your associations and

MMC

relationships. If the five people you spend the most time with have pretty similar personalities to one another, then that means your way of "familiar thinking" is most likely one form of thinking. It may also mean that you will not be as open-minded as someone who has five friends with diverse thoughts. Furthermore, this means that when you surround yourself with more friends who are creative and confident in what they do, you are bound to get that energy from them and transform it into yours too.

This is why being curious and open-minded is an important trait of being a creative. When you look at everything with curiosity, you are inclined to learn and understand more rather than simply accept things as they are. If this scares you, or makes your feel uneasy, ask yourself why. Understand that you may not necessarily need to gain all experiences directly to understand certain values, and that there are many things that you can learn indirectly if you permit yourself to keep an open mind.

REFLECT

To that point, try to engage an open and honest mind as you answer these questions:

* Who are the five people I spend the most time with at work? How are they similar? How are they different?

* When was the last time I felt curious in my work?

* As a leader, how can I ensure I receive input and gather perspectives from multiple resources instead of clinging to one?

* As a leader, how can I encourage my team members to look for new resources and information when problem-solving?

* As a company, how can we do a better job of

attracting talent that will bring diverse perspectives to our work?

✳ As a company, how might we continue to encourage our employees to stay open-minded?

Do you see any patterns in your responses? Are there any surprises? Why or why not? Your level of self-awareness plays a pivotal role in your creative thinking and your willingness to maintain an open mind.

APPLY

Let's take an honest look at your habits in your organization and within your team. Do the five people you spend the most time with in the office have similar personalities, ethnicities, and/or professional backgrounds? If they are not diverse, why aren't they? When you hold team meetings are there certain people that you consistently feel more comfortable opening up discussion with? Why?

Asking such questions at first can feel uncomfortable and even more so if you know that you have leaned toward one group or experience more than others. However, acknowledging that and being aware of your biases is the very first step of learning how to open up. Take a look at your answers with an eye of curiosity. Why do you see such patterns? Why do you think you haven't tried reaching out to new groups, making new friends, or immersing yourself in new experiences?

As a team leader, expanding your resources and learning is important because you'll want to ensure that you are not skewing your decision-making process and that you are providing space for your team members to open up. This takes both the courage to be honest about your thinking process and time to make these changes. Take a close look at the five people you rely on to make a decision. Why do you rely on them and not others? What experience or information do you tend to discount? Why? Spend time as part of each work day asking yourself these questions. It will be hard to create a space for others to be more open-minded if you are not walking the talk as a leader.

When I work with leaders who are struggling with this, I encourage them to make one simple change to the way they begin or run their meetings. Start with asking for your employees' opinions more and validating their perspectives and concerns. Remind them why you appreciate their contribution and how it made an impact. Saying something as simple as, "Thank you, [Name], for bringing up that point last time. Thanks to that insight, we changed our meeting structure that helped us get _____ result," or "Thank you, [Name], for sharing your suggestion on this. While we will not be implementing this due to limited resources, your insight inspired us to do _____ that will help us do _____. What do you think?" The public recognition and making the effort of getting to know them encourages others who have not spoken up yet to speak up. It also makes those who have feel heard, validated, and appreciated. Also consider trying a new question set from the open-ended question game like SPARK. Your team will start to open up and you'll be able to witness how each person in the room answers the questions in their unique way, giving them valuable time to get to know each other on a deeper level.

As a company, if you have diverse talent but see skewed team interaction, you'll want to strategize on intentional cross collaboration. Are there ways teams can authentically get to know each other and support one another? If not, what can you offer or create to ensure individuals are being exposed to different perspectives and personalities? Even if their friendships in a new department may not impact their deliverables, your employees will increase their awareness of the bigger picture and become more mindful of diverse workflow and perspectives in the office.

If you are concerned with not attracting or retaining diverse talent, you'll want to strategize in the hiring and recruitment phase as well as internal team interaction, management, and retention. Where are you going to find your talent, but more importantly, where are you not going to recruit new employees? Who are the individuals going out to recruit and how are they describing the company and job?

You cannot expect change when you are not changing

your methodologies or examining how your actions and inactions may be skewing your decision-making and management style.

RECAP

Your experiences and relationships influence what you define as "normal" versus "different." To be more creative, try opening yourself up to a larger breadth of connections and experiences, while consciously staying open-minded and curious. Create a team with diverse backgrounds. Learn new things outside your expertise. Ask more questions. And as you learn, stay open and appreciative of the diversity of thoughts. You do not have to agree or like everything new you try, but you don't want your fear hindering your potential.

Inside the InnovatorsBox®

SPARK is our signature creative card game series that empowers collaboration and communication. Learning how to think differently is important but can be hard if we have not done it in a while. SPARK question cards are divided into creativity, curiosity, and reflection to kindle your questioning and thinking and to challenge you to think differently. It's great for brainstorming, networking, team building, and getting to know yourself better. You can pick from two versions. SPARK 1 is the green box and SPARK 2 is the yellow box. SPARK 1 is good to start with if you are exploring creative questioning with your team for the first time. SPARK 2 is good if you have completed SPARK 1 and want additional challenging and creative questions.

Creativity is the act of thinking

DIFFERENTLY.

NOTES

3
THE BEST THINGS DON'T HAPPEN OVERNIGHT

"It takes 20 years to make an overnight success."
—EDDIE CANTOR
Comedian, Actor, Songwriter

We've heard it. We know it. But we still hesitate to understand and embrace the fact that the best things do not happen overnight. This may explain why we get frustrated when our delivery is ten minutes late or when we can't get back into shape fast enough. We feel like we've done enough hard work and we want to see the results right now. Despite the abundant research and success stories that show how success is built over time with dedication and patience, we often expect to reach our milestones faster. I understand this because I have been there more than I should have or care to admit. This is one area where augmented social media usage and technological advancement have not helped. As our access to information becomes easier, our expectation to get what we want with ease has skyrocketed while our patience overall has dramatically plunged.

So no wonder people find it difficult to embrace and practice creativity. Many are expecting to instantly become creative. They will inevitably be disappointed. They're underestimating the power of persistence, and what they can do if they put in consistent effort!

Imagine two scenarios: Scenario A where you have exercised once in three months for four hours. Scenario B where you have exercised for 20 minutes, three times a week, for three months. Which scenario would lead you to better health? Most likely scenario B. That's not hard to understand. We know that doing something consistently with dedication and attention is powerful and more impactful than putting in a lot of effort just once. That's why those who practice their craft more regularly perform better than those who put in one huge effort.

Building a creative mindset works the same way. It's no different than how physical muscles work. When you flex your creative muscles more frequently and with intention, you become stronger. The qualitative quantity makes a difference. This is why doing sprints of a task with full focus is more impactful than multitasking two or more deliverables. Our brains get scattered and we can't dive as deeply into solving one problem as we otherwise would with full focus.

In an office setting, this means it will take time and practice to discover and implement the best ways to build a creative culture, team, and product or service that fits with your company. The number one mistake I observe when working with my clients is how they respond to creativity when things don't happen fast enough or in the form they had in mind. They stop the creative process—as fast as they can. Once that message is sent, it is harder to regain the trust and input from your employees. Why should they put extra effort and energy in programs, initiatives or problem-solving only to feel punished when the results aren't fast enough? It's a fair question to ask before you simply blame your people for not acting in a way that is in direct alignment with your expectations. When they see that leadership is not open to how creativity can be expressed in different ways, they are less likely to open up and propose new ideas. Why bring up new suggestions if the leadership says no every time someone suggests something?

I certainly understand the importance of being mindful of your limited resources and time as a company, whether you are a for-profit or nonprofit, but giving little space for the people to grow by experiencing trial and error is shortsighted. If there is no space to test without the fear of being blamed, why would anyone try something?

Think about a child. Do you blame a newborn for not running when he or she is still learning how to crawl? Do you discourage him or her from attempting to walk since he or she keeps falling down or tripping? No. Neither do we blame nor discourage because we know it is a natural process. We understand that with practice and trust the child will learn how to walk, run, and do more. So why do we expect every team to jump before learning how to crawl in creativity?

Similarly expecting your teams to think of creative solutions all the time and finding the best one in a single attempt is unrealistic. Expecting them to be constantly creative because you provide vacation time, training, or a comfortable workspace, complete with snacks, is unrealistic. Those resources can contribute to an employee's emotional state at work, but giving these benefits with a high expectation will only pressure them and make them see innovation as "one more thing I need to do" instead of seeing the opportunity to create as fun.

Think about the last policy or program you put in place to boost your team's creativity. What did you offer and what was your reaction when things did not go as planned? Did you take that offering away? How did you communicate your expectations and goals? How did your people respond to you? As an employee, think about how you felt when your company expressed interest in prioritizing creativity or innovation. Did you feel like you had the time to be more creative? Why or why not?

Learning when to pivot when things do not go well is

important, but learning how to take the time to nurture and explore is also important. Since it takes time to figure out what is the best way, you need to start with approaches that are workable with your budget, company goals, and timelines. Starting with something small and consistent is more important than doing something flashy and taking it away if you don't see the result in a few days.

REFLECT

Here are questions to help you brainstorm ways to provide the time and the space for trial and error as you work to find the best creative approaches:

* How can I incorporate creativity into my daily routine at work—even when I'm busy?

* How could I have approached a recent challenge with a customer, client, or a colleague differently?

* As a team leader, how can I encourage my team members to practice creative thinking and creative problem-solving?

* As a team leader, how can I make creativity fun and not another task for my team members?

* As a company, how can we empower leaders to prioritize creative thinking even if it takes time and trial and error?

* As a company, what is the safe boundary we can provide that will not hurt the company's financial and resource constraints?

APPLY

First, I want to gently remind you to not be too hard on yourself for not accomplishing the creative goals in the way or at the pace you wanted to. It's supposed to take time, practice, and trial and error. It's okay to fail and make mistakes. You will learn from it. And it's okay that certain things may take more time than you thought. If reconnecting with our creative selves was easy we would have figured this out a long time ago!

I used to think that I was being hard on myself because I feared disappointing others, but in truth it was really on me. I was the harshest critic because I disliked the feeling of failing. So I started to do two things that helped me focus on the marathon instead of seeing things as a sprint to the finish line. First, I sought out inspiring stories of individuals, companies, and teams that overcame challenges and became successful. Look at how Jack Ma built Alibaba, Walt Disney built the Walt Disney Company, or Oprah Winfrey built The Oprah Winfrey Network (OWN). Their companies are here today not because they expected to reach their goals in one day, but because of a vision they were not willing to give up. Reading, listening, and watching these real stories remind me that I am not alone and that expecting my creativity hack to work in three days (or less!) is nonsense. There is power in what we read, listen, and see. The more I expose myself to these stories the more I embed that thinking into my life.

Second, I take more time to reflect and forgive myself. Every time I experience disappointment with myself I take a moment to pause, slowly count to 10 so that I don't rush into any decisions or emotions, tell myself that it's okay, and ask with curiosity, "What did I learn about myself through this experience?" Those few minutes help me focus on the learning instead of blaming. It also reminds me to enjoy the process more than hesitating with fear and falling off track. At times, I still find myself unconsciously flustered when I cannot get certain things fast enough, but learning how to do this has helped me be a better problem solver, communicator, and collaborator.

As a team leader, how you lead, communicate, and respond to failure, errors, and new initiatives will impact how your team members collaborate, create, and initiate. As the leader of the group, in addition to walking the talk, it is essential you are the bodyguard and protector of your group's creative space. Don't just tell them that you are there to support them. Show them so that they know that they can open up, take risks, and know that you are on their side even if it takes some time or if the idea fails.

Here's how:

First, take the opportunity to clearly define the boundaries of time, resources, and action scope that are acceptable for your team members to experiment within. Whether that is using new Excel forms or using digital tools instead of paper, clearly defining what is easily experimentable will help them understand what they can explore. It will also ensure you are following your company's core goals, values, and priorities.

Next, make it a practice to acknowledge the positive lessons learned from failed initiatives, as well as from the successful ones. When we only highlight the successes, we run the risk of discouraging an attempt at something new out of fear that it won't be as good as our last effort. To get people comfortable with consistently sharing new ideas or trying new projects and initiatives, it is important to create a practice of reflecting as a group and a team and defining the lessons learned.

Finally, when setting the definition and expectation around creativity and innovation, encourage the team to work on building more frequent small wins together instead of perfecting one solution. When your team members understand that you appreciate every small milestone, they are going to get more comfortable talking about the small wins and attempting the big wins. But if they feel pressured to only think of big wins, they may be discouraged from taking the first step.

I also encourage you to think of utilizing your physical office spaces and existing business routines. Is there a place that you can designate as a creative zone and let your employees be free to do and create what they want a little differently? You can symbolize that creativity zone through decorations, by placing helpful tools and items in the room, or by being selective and methodical about the type of events you hold there. Also consider providing your employees with the opportunity to get out of the office by attending retreats, educational programs, or workshops. The key is to always start small and to pair any creative strategy with positive reinforcement.

RECAP

There is no such thing as overnight success. Constant practice and the availability of intentional space to create are essential. And what you choose to believe will impact what you achieve. When you choose to see that it is impossible, it will remain an impossible task. Same with innovation. If you want real innovation, be ready to put in the work. Make creativity a part of your habit and practice it more frequently. Only intentional creativity will yield concrete results at work and in your life.

Inside the InnovatorsBox®

How might I...

Asking questions is great. Asking open-ended questions is essential. If you are unsure where to start, try using the "How might I" question approach. This one often will help you stay open-minded as it does not lead you to forming a yes or no answer. This is why this term is often used in design thinking or innovation programing. You can push yourself and your team to think differently by posing more "How might I" questions in the work routine.

Make it a practice to acknowledge the positive lessons learned from failed initiatives,

as well as from the successful ones.

NOTES

4
CONSTRAINTS—
YOUR NEW
BEST FRIEND

"But out of limitation comes creativity."
—DEBBIE ALLEN
Actress, Choreographer

What is your first, knee-jerk reaction to tough situations and challenges at work? Do you procrastinate, delay making decisions, or complain to your colleagues? OR do you express gratitude and excitement for the opportunity to test your skills and flex your creative mindset?

Not many of us are exactly thrilled when we face unpleasant surprises, difficult situations, and complicated problems. It's one thing to watch a movie and read stories about other people overcoming a tough period and being inspired by it. But it's completely another to be the one in the story. In the past, I have definitely felt unprepared, ill-equipped, exhausted, or stressed (or all of the above), because I had no idea when I would get to the end of "the tunnel." Or if there was an end at all.

What if I tell you that this is **the** prime time to be creative?

I know you want to shake your head in denial. It does not feel logical. But this is the very reason it works. Creativity is not logical. You are supposed to find something new out of existing resources or circumstances. That's why it sometimes feels weird or tense. We are more likely to discover unexpected solutions in high pressure situations because it is unlikely that we can solve them in the usual ways. At the end of the day, that's where we find the unexpected answers.

I've seen this again and again when I do creative exercises in my workshops and speaking sessions. The best, most wild ideas often come at the very end of the session when I tell the group that they have 20 seconds left. While they feel tense with the limited time, they also share how often this pushes them to let go of expectations of perfection and hesitation in order to focus on delivering. Prioritizing *doing* over *thinking* permits them to think of pretty cool ideas that bring critical insights and new directions—better than the ones they thought of when they had a lot more time.

Think about it. They had the same resources, they are the same people, but they had a harder time thinking about an innovative idea at the beginning because they still had a lot of time to overthink and stop themselves from being too silly.

Let's look at a real example you can relate to. Think of the last time you did something brilliant and creative. What was that moment like? I'm guessing you probably had to tie different information, knowledge, and experience into addressing the problem. You probably had to add a bit of creativity to think of something different. But ultimately, you still had to choose one way to tackle it. That decision you made was probably defined by limited time, resources, and other constraints. You also probably knew that out of all your ideas, you had to choose one.

Ruth Noller, a creative researcher in 1950s, beautifully explains this in her creativity formula.

C = f(x)(K, I, and E)

The form of **(C)** creativity is based on **K** (knowledge), **I** (imagination), and **E** (evaluation). No matter how many good ideas, or how imaginative you are, if you are not making a decision or taking action, your innovative thoughts will stay as ideas—they will not flourish. And knowing that innovation is born out of creativity, you can't be innovative without constraints.

This is why companies are discovering how putting time and budget constraints on a project can be an eye-opening experience. In fact, a friend tried this and was excited to see the result. She told her team that they had six months to work on a project and had less than $50,000 to spend. Everyone thought she was crazy. Traditionally projects of the scope she had in mind in the technical industry would take two years and easily $1 million. But she did not have the time and needed to find a working solution—fast. Her team members complained saying that it was impossible. But she promised two things that helped change the narrative, "I have your back and you can change some of the rules to get there." Did they reach their goal? Yes, in fact they spent $10,000 less than what they originally expected and the working prototype was immediately implemented in the factory. As a result of this experiment, the company has changed the way they develop prototypes, which has hugely impacted their company's productivity, product development, and revenue. Was it a risk? Yes. Could she have put forward an impossible demand? Yes. But without trying something like this you will never know what is possible. So trying something small and experimenting with different constraints is a critical start.

Let's look further.

Most innovations were born out of challenges. The difference was that unlike those who complained, these innovators used their energy to solve problems instead, and looked at the challenge at hand as an opportunity to advance.

Try this exercise with me to see if that is true.

Write down three products that changed the way you live today.

Next, write down three companies that you highly admire, and even use their services or products with joy.

Now, let's do a little research. Look them up and see how they started. I bet all of them originated from a strong resolve to change a tough situation or to solve a problem. I also bet many of them did not exist or were considered weird for what they were proposing, as it was too new for most people to comprehend. If you are looking to be more creative, you have to learn how to work with constraints and enjoy the challenges, not see them as threats.

The attitude toward constraints is why I disagree with leaders who express the lack of resource abundance to be their reason for lack of creativity in the office. I cannot emphasize enough that your constraints are your biggest gifts to being creative because they push you to bring new ideas to the table and to make better decisions. If you have ever associated creativity with resource abundance, this is your cue to realize that you've got creativity all wrong.

Abundant resources, in fact, can be the enemy to creativity. Yes, you may be able to do more, but you must never confuse *having more expensive options* with *pursuing creative approaches.* This is why experts, artists, and innovative companies have purposely put constraints into place to make more creative decisions, build creative products, and build a creative community. Musicians like Bob Dylan purposely take out certain beats or use only two rhythms to first test what music they can create. Writers like Dr. Seuss[2] put word limits to create masterpieces like *The Cat in the Hat.* If you find the right balance of pressure and challenge, you can use that as a way to push yourself further.

However, it is important to remember that not all challenges can trigger innovation—even with good intention. This is because the human brain, while limitless, gets tired and needs time to rest and pause. Science says that adults make about 35,000 conscious decisions a day[3] (some days we do even more). Children, by contrast, only make about 3,000. No wonder we felt less stressed when we were younger. We make about 226.7 decisions each day on food alone, and when we combine everything we do, think, say, and feel every day, this absurd number actually stacks up. But when we exceed 35,000 decisions on any given day, we start experiencing "decision fatigue." When we have decision fatigue, the quality of our decisions deteriorates rapidly. Our decisions become more impulsive, and our ability to self-regulate is impaired. In other words, no matter how creative or smart you are, when you are experiencing decision fatigue, you are not your best self.

This is an important factor to know because if you are making too many decisions and trying to solve a lot of complicated problems all at once, even the most creative people have tendencies to perform poorly. So, what do you do? To get the most out of those challenges, you have to give yourself space to pause, reflect, and rest. The moment you try to outperform every single moment is the moment you are not letting your creative engine perform at its best. Sure, it needs practice, but it also needs to pause and take a step back.

REFLECT

How are you doing so far? Let's recap with some questions:

* How do I respond to on-the-job challenges? Why do I react that way? How can I approach the next challenge with more curiosity and an open mind?

* How can I practice creating constrained spaces to enhance creativity?

* How can I create constraints in my organization/

team/department to enhance creativity as a group?

✱ How might I make time to pause/reflect/rest so that I bring my best creative work to my position?

✱ As a team leader, how will I ensure my team members don't become overly decision fatigued? How will I support them when they get burned out or become exhausted by decision fatigue?

As a company, what are ways we can inspire employees to practice constraints without being judged or poorly evaluated?

APPLY

No constraint and challenge are the same. Nor are they approached in the same way. It is critical to have an honest conversation with yourself to learn how to get comfortable with constraints, as well as knowing your limits before you hit decision fatigue.

As you have noticed from the earlier chapters, self-reflection and self-awareness play key roles in strengthening your reaction to challenges. It's okay for you to recognize that you detest getting last-minute requests, changes, or time constraints that make you end the day with a heavy sigh. I am not saying that you may enjoy the experience of fighting constraints the way you may enjoy a vacation day under the sun. But knowing all of that is still significantly more helpful than not knowing. Instead of being reactive, you can choose to be proactive when responding to these challenges.

Let's try this three-step activity together.

FIRST, look back at the last five incidents at work when you felt frustrated or stressed about a constraint or challenge. Write down all the details related to the incidents—who was involved, when did it happen, what caused it, how was it communicated, why did it happen, how did you respond, and why did you feel that way?

SECOND, see if you can find a pattern. As you honestly map out and reflect your last few instances, you may notice that there are particular times, individuals, or moments that trigger you more than others. No matter how obvious this may be, write it down. Be honest. This will help you identify both your triggers in constraint and your habitual reactions. Did you find the patterns? Unless you take this step, it will be hard to know how to adjust your response, and how to prepare for the next incident!

THIRD, based on these patterns, determine what things you can change. Consider asking your colleagues to consider making a few adjustments in how they work with you as a way to improve the constraint utilization. This step of communication and change is key. Awareness will help you be alert but without taking action to change the way you think, respond, and communicate with others' constraints will easily push you to fatigue.

Let me share an example with my personal story.

In my personal reflection with constraints, I noticed three patterns that get me upset. First, when new constraints such as deadlines, limited resources, or change in work scope directly impact the deliverables that I worked so hard to put together. I became unhappy with the unexpected changes because it felt like I could no longer deliver my best work. I felt like I would be evaluated and judged on work that I did not want to present, which meant I would now have to spend more of my own time after work to get my deliverables done. That thought worried me.

My second trigger is when imposed constraints, without a clear explanation, would impact my deliverables. In addition to impacting my work, this made me feel left out. If a time constraint was given, I did not know why. If a resource was suddenly taken away, there was no explanation to why. I realized that these moments made me feel unprepared and weakened my ability to problem-solve because I did not know the full context of why we were changing course.

My last trigger is the constraints created by upper management that seem to go in the opposite direction of my recommendations. It made me question why I would take the time to bring up an idea. It also discouraged me from wanting to think of new ideas: Why bother if management is not willing to listen or change?

Am I touching on something similar to what you may have experienced? Yes, unfortunately, my experience is similar to that of many employees in any organization. What I learned from identifying those three patterns was how important communication, clarification, and building trust was. When those three elements were not in place, all challenges and constraints felt harder to handle. When those three elements were planted, challenges did not feel as bad. Just like your muscles aching after a good workout, it felt natural.

So instead of complaining about my triggers, I took action!

I scheduled a meeting with my manager to express my concerns and to ask what I could do to better understand his perspective. I asked for tangible actions we both could take so that we could communicate better and in a way that worked for us both. And most importantly, we promised to trust each other. Instead of reacting to the constraint, I agreed to trust that there was a reason for him to make the decision. This trust-building process was not solved in one meeting, but it significantly improved our productivity and collaboration over time.

I started seeking more clarification of the bigger picture and eagerly asked why more constraints were being introduced. Attitude is key. Whether this is your supervisor or colleague, when we seek to better understand why certain things are done a certain way it helps us understand and create new solutions.

I learned to give myself more time to respond and to make decisions. While completing deliverables quickly is critical, these experiences helped me recognize speedy results without deeper understanding will not bring the same result. Even if it's five more minutes, that time spent thinking and wanting to understand why that constraint was created gave my colleague and me the space to tackle and solve it.

None of this was solved in one meeting, but the consistent effort and initiative helped us find trusted ground and find new ways to solve tough problems together. You shouldn't have to wait until your manager, colleague, or your intern reaches out to talk with you. When we proactively step up to show that we care to make this work together, they will appreciate it.

As a leader, the above example should be something to think about in how you manage and communicate with your team. What are you doing to proactively create that communication and building a space of trust? I understand taking the time to meet with everyone over every concern will take more time when things are already busy, but try changing your mindset by seeing this as a grounded investment. It is so much easier to face the tough days when your team knows that you have their back, and when you know that they have each other's backs. How are you communicating that? How are you walking that talk? How are you helping your company cultivate that space by looking out for your team members? Are you stepping up for your team members when other managers try to point fingers and blame your team members? All of your actions matter. At the end of the day we are all human, and that includes you and your team members.

Just like for an individual, it is key for the company to reflect and think about what challenges mean to them. What are the constraints that are extremely difficult to walk through? What are the losses that you can handle? When we are aware of the manageable challenges and constraints we can learn how to prepare for them and how to communicate about them with your people. Not every challenge is a major emergency nor should it be. Don't put your people in extreme pressure every single day. Sooner or later that will burn them out. Think about the boy who cried wolf!

Instead, take the time to see how amazing it is to see people glow and become energized—no matter the challenge—when they work in companies that they know have their back and the space to be creative.

Always keep in mind that your people are your company's greatest resources. Are people happy to come to work or are they "working for the weekend"? Why do they enjoy tackling one problem after another with you?

Be a company that embraces challenges with your people. Together you can go far.

Embrace challenges and constraints. Look at them as opportunities to improve, solve a problem, and be creative. Create opportunities where you can intentionally practice your creativity by purposely placing time and resource constraints on your assignments. Know when you have to take a step back and rest.

Inside the InnovatorsBox®

SCAMPER

A great tool to practice thinking differently in a structured way, SCAMPER was proposed by Alex Osborn in 1953 and was further developed by Bob Eberle in 1971. SCAMPER is an activity-based thinking process that can be performed by cooperative learning. First define the topic you want to work on and the ideas and goals you had related to it. Then choose one of the options in SCAMPER to see how your ideas and thoughts change as a result of it. For instance:

→ *SUBSTITUTE* is coming up with another topic that is equivalent to the present topic

→ *COMBINE* is adding information to the original topic

→ *ADJUST* is identifying ways to construct the topic

→ *MODIFY* is creatively changing the topic

→ *PUT TO OTHER USES* is identifying possible scenarios and situations where this topic can be used

→ *ELIMINATE* is removing ideas or elements from the topic that are not valuable

→ *REVERSE AND REARRANGE* is evolving a new concept from the original concept

---

Forced Application

You can't force someone to be instantly creative but you can certainly use prompts to spark different thinking. Forced application is the process of using two unusual ideas, elements, or products and being forced to see what new ideas come from the relationship. This approach is a good way to practice thinking how everything has an opportunity to spark something new. For instance, if you have a black pen and an unopened chocolate bar, think of all the ways you can make a new product for elderly healthcare. Perhaps the chocolate inspires you to create something that is brown or chewy or comes in a bar shape. Perhaps the pen inspires you to document things or discover how to connect the two items in a unique way. Both objects can help inspire you to find new elements and think differently. The more random the objects are from one another the better.

Think of the last time you did something brilliant and creative.

What was that moment like?

NOTES

5
THE POWER OF KNOWING YOUR TRUE SELF

*"Knowing others is wisdom,
knowing yourself is enlightenment."*

—LAO TZU
Philosopher, Writer

When my corporate clients complain that their teams are not creative and are underperforming, I look back at Sun Tzu's *The Art of War*[4] and reflect upon this quote I love:

"If you know the enemy and know yourself,
you need not fear the result of a hundred battles.
If you know yourself but not the enemy,
for every victory gained you will also suffer a defeat.

If you know neither the enemy nor yourself,
you will succumb in every battle."

Sun Tzu is describing the power of self-awareness.
While Tzu is referring to a military context, this kind of
analysis works in any life situation. The more you know your
strengths, weaknesses, habits, and triggers for stress and joy,
the more you can make better decisions and solve problems
effectively, because you are utilizing all your insights and
possibilities. And the more you are aware of the challenge,
the better you can tackle it. This is a critical element of the
creative mindset because if you are self-aware, it also means
that you will know what you need to be inspired, what you
need to avoid, and when you need to pause to be creative.

Unfortunately, most adults do not spend enough time
studying oneself and may never fully know what they could
have done in their lifetime. This is why leaders without
self-awareness make decisions that can put companies or
families at risk.

Artist Candy Chang[5] reminded us of this when she
launched the "Before I Die" public art project in her New
Orleans neighborhood in 2011. She lost someone she loved
and she wanted to remember the importance of living
without regret. She painted the side of an abandoned house
with chalkboard paint and stenciled the sentence, "Before
I die I want to_____." Within a day the wall was full with
honest confessions from neighbors who shared all the things
they regretted not doing. It was a powerful reflection of how
often we do things out of fear as well as a way to recognize
that there is still hope, that there is still time. Taking a
moment to acknowledge our regret is a powerful way of
moving forward. Since then, she has found similar messages
from people all over the world through the four hundred
walls she has created. This means many people are living
each day with regret. They are not doing the things they
really wish—or want—to do.

What about you? Will you be on your deathbed with
more regret or satisfaction for all the paths you've taken?
How can you learn to be more self-aware, to fully get to know
the real you?

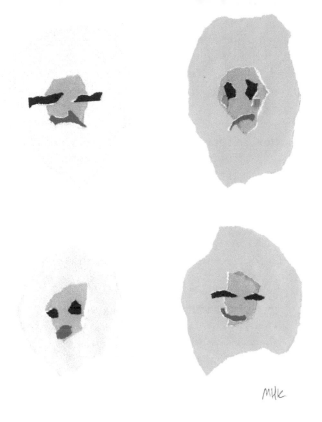

MHK

If you posed these questions to the younger Monica Kang, I would have answered with confidence how I lived every day to the fullest and that I knew myself very well. I was organized. I kept a journal. I had a plan for my future and I was doing everything I could to live a step closer to making that vision come to life. What I forgot to enjoy was what was happening in the moment. As a career-driven high achiever, I focused on defining my todays based on what I wanted to see tomorrow. It also meant I spent less time focused on how to make the most out of each day for the sake of each day. I worked hard but I did not understand how to play hard or the importance of it.

"What do you do for fun?" I remember pausing a lot longer than I needed to when someone asked me this as a student. "Your hobbies?"

I remember walking home that night in a state of shock. I could not remember the last time I did anything for fun—

just to have fun and not to add to my resume. I started dissecting my motives: Am I posting this article because I want to get likes or because I really want to share and express something? Am I taking this job because it will look good on my resume even if I don't enjoy this type of work? Am I building a life based on what others expect or want from me?

Somehow, as I got older, it felt harder to spend time doing things just for fun since I wanted to be serious about my life. I didn't want hobbies distracting me from building a great career. I didn't realize I was taking a step further away from my true self and my creativity. How would I live a fulfilling life if I never took the time to explore what inspired, motivated, and energized me?

Knowing now who my favorite singers, books, travel destinations, and restaurants are has helped me realize my favorite ways to communicate, do projects, and work with teams. And understanding what I need, want, and like has helped me learn how to express, seek, and communicate those to colleagues, mentors, and my supervisors. The attitude of "let me make the best out of each moment" has helped me find new answers in unexpected places and decrease burnout in the face of challenges. Knowing who I am has helped me find a way to express and let myself out. I stopped feeling trapped in my own thoughts and feeling evaluated by everyone. Because the only person truly evaluating my progress is me:

아는 사람은 좋아하는 사람만 못하고, 좋아하는 사람은 즐기는 사람만 못하다. - 공자 -
知之者 不如好之者 好之者 不如樂之者

*"Those who simply know can't reach as far
as those who like something,
Those who simply like it cannot reach as far
as those who truly enjoy each moment."*
—CONFUCIUS
Philosopher, Politician

My English translation of this phrase does not justify how simple and powerful it is to enjoy living life instead of knowing what it means to enjoy. This is why I am hugely inspired by artists, leaders, and speakers who pour their enthusiasm and full effort into their work. Their joy in creating is so contagious that I find myself smiling as if I am in the same room with them. And it works for all mediums. When we do any action with sincerity and joy, our expression reflects on our creation. You can not only enjoy what you create, but you can potentially inspire someone. That's powerful.

How about you? Are you spending each moment with sincerity and passion? When was the last time you did not care how much time passed working on something because you enjoyed it so much? As a leader, when was the last time you noticed your team felt fully energized working and coming to work?

REFLECT

Here are some questions to help you get to know yourself at work, and how to better get to know your employees:

* What are my superpowers? What is my Achilles heel?

* What does it look like to bring 100% to my work and to my life?

* What is stopping me from bringing my 100%? Is it changeable or improvable?

* As a team leader, what can I do to help my team members feel comfortable enough to be themselves?

* As a team leader, how can I lead as an example for the team?

* As a company, how might I encourage my employees to bring their unique traits into the office without fear of being judged?

* As a company, how do we define our authentic creative culture?

Imagine if more people came to the office feeling their 100% and performing 100%! Not only would we have better products and better service delivery, but we'd also have happier and less stressed people at work. We would also see more diverse and creative thoughts blossoming around us since every person's 100% version is different. The best part is, regardless of what tier you stand on in your company, you can make this change for yourself AND your team. So, stop feeling limited right from this moment.

APPLY

The challenge is that excellence in the workplace does not always equal us being our 100%. Not everyone is in a job that they feel their 100% in, nor are they with a team that makes them feel their 100%. Your circumstances may make you feel as though asking for such moments is unimaginable. I do understand what that can feel like. I used to work in nuclear nonproliferation as a government contractor. It was not necessarily the most creative industry, but I still found a way to bring out my 100% value in the most routine role. Yes, you heard it. I found a way to be creative with Excel sheets, emails, and meetings. And that made a significance difference in how I felt about my work. I took very small, intentional steps.

I was surprised to find myself singing songs with joy in my head even when doing boring, routine tasks such as Excel documenting. Everything was so much more fun because I focused on bringing my best self to each task. After putting in the hours and building my creative mindset, no task felt meaningless or boring. Every moment became an adventure that I had yet to tackle. Every challenge felt like a new puzzle that I had not solved. I started to excel at work and as a result, I brought greater value—not because I focused on bringing more value, but because I wanted to focus on making the most out of every moment in my day.

Let me explain.

As a manager, you have the opportunity to create a safe space for your team to be creative and bring out their 100% through leading by example and changing the work dynamic. But in order to do that, you need to know yourself and bring out that authentic version of yourself in the office. Add humor, honesty, and a piece of who you are as a person in your meetings. While it is important to go through your agenda, it is equally as important for your team members to get a sense of who you are as a person. This makes your team feel open, safe, and comfortable to be themselves.

In addition to injecting yourself into the equation, think about how you can engage your team members:

✻ Do you ask creative questions?

✻ Do you spend a few minutes learning about what everyone else is doing?

✻ Do you spend a few minutes sharing your biggest challenges and the accomplishments that you are most proud of?

✻ Is there an intentional space that allows your team to get to know each other's strengths and weaknesses and to celebrate the differences and similarities?

Reflecting on these questions and putting these simple practices into action can be powerful for collaboration, productivity, efficiency, and most importantly, their accountability to one another.

As an employee, you may have to take the bottoms-up approach. Try not to get discouraged as you work to get to know and express yourself. You may be in a company that will discourage you from bringing 100% of yourself to work (because they think you are being weird or unprofessional), but please do not let that stop you from discovering who you are and what you can achieve. Once you get to know yourself, identify your strengths, and become aware of what inspires you, you will start to see how you can logically and strategically bring that out in your work. Maybe it's in the way you communicate with others. Maybe it's in how you operate in the office. Whatever it is, find it, and start doing things that will help you be limitless and bring out your best self, regardless of the task at hand. Let the results shine. When the managers see the positive results of your unique "quirks" they will be happy.

If your manager is still not receptive to your positive attempts, look for other allies. Are there managers, colleagues, or individuals who you respect and who support you? If you do not find them in your own organization, are there people in your industry or in your network? Knowing that you have people who will help you and encourage you to stay true in or near the office can be a positive influence despite the internal challenges.

Furthermore, if you find a way to express your 100% at work in whatever small way, you will feel more liberated and less stressed. It's exhausting when you have to bring a different version of yourself to any situation. Don't wait for an opportunity to express yourself—seek it out!

Understanding why curating a space for your people to bring your 100% is even more critical when you look at how our workplace is changing. The factory assembly-line approach of hiring someone to do one thing in a chain of steps is no longer realistic. Both companies and workforces are demanding a different way of working. Why we work and how we find good talent is changing. Companies are looking for talent that is flexible, proactive, and able to problem-solve and innovate. People are also looking to work on what they love, care about, and can grow with. A larger part of the workforce is choosing to not work in a traditional career. They are working as freelancers, small business owners, and sub-contractors in order to hone their skills, work on projects they love, and enjoy a certain sense of freedom. Perhaps one day we will have careers without working in one company full time. In the meantime, for companies to attract and retain the talent they need to grow and thrive, it is essential to give employees the creative space they require.

RECAP

The more we know about ourselves the more we can bring out our best and creative selves. Ask more questions and reflect to practice self-awareness.

NOTES

6
YOUR BEST TOOLS ARE ROOTED IN CURIOSITY

"I think, at a child's birth, if a mother could ask a fairy godmother to endow it with the most useful gift, that gift should be curiosity."

—ELEANOR ROOSEVELT
Politician, Diplomat, Activist

"The important thing is not to stop questioning. Curiosity has its own reason for existing."

—ALBERT EINSTEIN
Physicist, Scientist

Understanding is one thing. Doing is entirely another. Despite everything we've discussed, some of you may still be itching to find a perfectly formulated solution that you can just take and replicate. We like to see results as soon as we can. Conversations and dialogues... why do all of that when you can ask Google for the answer or order it on Amazon?

While technology has given us an advantage to access information with ease, it has also killed a bit of our willingness to explore, think, and be curious, which are key ingredients to creativity. I never forgot how a friend of mine always responded to every question I asked with, "Just ask Google." We got our answers, but we also stopped having conversations.

Unfortunately, our hunger for the "perfect solution" is familiar and understandable. We have been trained this way for a large part of our life. We have been told to follow prospective paths and get results so much that we stopped asking questions or wondering why we do things a certain way. Take a look back at our school days where we spent a large amount of time filling in the correct bubble or finding a right way to write an essay that would get us the scores we needed to get into the right school. Or take a good look at your office where you are expected to follow the exact instructions and processes to reach a certain outcome which leaves little room for newer approaches to get to that result.

This is why psychologists like Warren Berger and Sir Ken Robinson have highlighted the danger of our current education and workforce patterns that are still treating humans as factory-workers. While work culture and style have changed since the factory ages, educational institutions still take a very standardized approach to learning, "The fact is that given the challenges we face, education doesn't need to be reformed—it needs to be transformed. The key to this transformation is not to standardize education, but to personalize it, to build achievement on discovering the individual talents of each child, to put students in an environment where they want to learn and where they can naturally discover their true passions," Ken Robinson, *The Element: How Finding Your Passion Changes Everything.*[6]

Similarly, in his book *A More Beautiful Question*, Warren Berger[7] shares how even children who start out asking hundreds of questions a day start to "fall off a cliff" and stop questioning and wondering as they enter school and, later as adults, the business world. Out of fear of being judged and being seen as wrong we stop wanting to try something different unless we know it is going to work.

So is there any hope to change this way of thinking?

First of all, call it out when you notice it. Acknowledging that you are not giving yourself time to think and reflect is an example of practicing self-awareness and courage. Be aware when you start to itch for that "perfect solution" or for instant results without giving any time to think things through. And also when you are being more willing to dive into thinking and reflecting. Being creative may be a natural human talent, but we didn't say it was easy.

Find out how you like to learn best and root it in curiosity. Are you a visual learner? Do you remember better through experience or through writing? Just like we are all creative differently, we are also naturally wired to enjoy learning differently. Understanding your preference for how you like to digest new information and craft your skills can be powerful. However, one key element to any form of learning and practicing creativity is **curiosity.**

When we are curious, we ask questions, we wonder, we pause, and we ask again. Through this process, we first learn something new, then we make it a habit, and then we embrace it—instead of doing something simply because we are told to do.

What about in organizations? Before you criticize your people for not being creative or innovative, look at your company culture and your management style. Are they overwhelmed with deliverables and deadlines that permit little space to think differently? How do you respond when they make mistakes? Do you give room for curious questioning so they can better understand how to complete a task? Or do you react negatively when they ask questions or request more time?

I'm reminded of the importance of curiosity when I'm leading creative workshops for InnovatorsBox®. From the most innovative Fortune 500 companies to legacy companies, many—despite leadership's good intention—are unaware of how overworked their people are. When you

overwork your people you risk not only burning them out but also giving little space to think, let alone think differently. Tasks become more reactive than proactive. They feel like they have no time to breathe. No wonder they prefer the "this has worked before approach" and "stay with the status quo." Why risk doing something new and being embarrassed or burned out?

One thing we do to help leadership recognize this problem is by doing creative exercises that force participants to think differently. For instance, we ask them to use a crayon to sketch their opinion instead of writing a memo or using a PowerPoint presentation. When participants do unfamiliar things in familiar places, they are reminded that even the smallest change can help them think differently and find new solutions.

In fact, studies show that curiosity makes learning even boring things more fun and effective. For instance, researchers from the University of California, Davis found in 2014[8] that curiosity prepares our brain for learning and makes subsequent learning more rewarding.

Take a look at Google's innovation formula:

Discovery + Collaboration + Fun =

INNOVATION

While having a fun, collaborative environment can build a creative culture, the importance of discovery is something that often slips out of our grip. Do not let that happen. The discovery and sense of curiosity can be added to the smallest routine or to the most visible office space for your employees and teams to stay hungry to learn and be open-minded.

Remember this is not a competition. This is not about how you can generate more ideas than your colleague Jack can. Or how you can illustrate something better than your friend Sarah. We are all bringing unique values to the table. Comparing ourselves with others is like comparing apples and oranges. Of course, you will get different results. The only comparison should be between your past, present, and future.

REFLECT

Did I get you thinking a bit deeper? Good. Here are some questions to continue asking and reflecting upon to bring more curiosity into your routine:

✳ How might I stay curious during my work routine at the office?

✳ What are three new questions you could ask about your deliverables?

✳ What would I do differently if I had less time/resources/help for this project?

* As a leader, how might I encourage my team members to stay curious and open-minded about the projects they work on?

* As a leader, what can I do to create a fun and curious work environment for my team members?

* As a company, how are we fostering spaces for people to pause and ask questions without feeling judged?

* As a company, how are we encouraging your leadership to proactively solve problems instead of reacting even when things get busy?

APPLY

As an individual, it is critical to take a proactive approach in creating a fun and curious day for yourself. Don't wait until your supervisor asks you questions to think about and react to it. Make intentional time to get to know what intrigues you, energizes you, excites you, and bores you.

For instance, I adore K-pop and musicals, so I often start my day with a series of soundtracks that will get me in a positive, high-energy mood. Even starting the day with one song that gets me going with higher energy is better than not listening to anything. And when I fall in love with a new song or soundtrack, I get extremely curious about the artists. So I research everything I can find about them—their journey, why they started doing music, what people say about them, how they present themselves, what they plan to do in the future. Learning more about their stories often lets me appreciate, and be inspired by, the songs even more.

I found that I apply a similar process to my work. Whether it is a new or routine task, I find that I have more fun when I feel like an explorer or a detective. I trick myself into problem-solving the most mundane Excel document and tell myself what I would do differently if I had to solve this case ten times faster, or in ten steps or less. This gets me into the practice of putting together lists of questions that I want to ask myself and my colleagues, and it reminds me in the future if I take on a similar task.

When working with colleagues, this approach gives me the space to give my colleagues the benefit of doubt. If someone takes more time than usual on deliverables that impact my work flow, instead of being upset, I wonder why and ask how I can help make the process easier. Those pauses and openness permits the space for me and my colleagues to often have conversations to better understand how to work together and bring better results. When you know that you are in control of how you experience your day, it is empowering and exciting.

If it has been a while since you were curious about something, set small goals and time to measure your progress and rediscover your interests:

First, find a place in your work routine where you can reflect on one question a day. This will help you practice questioning with an open mind:

1] What do I spend most of my time doing in the office?

2] What do I enjoy doing the most in the office? Why? How can I make time to do at least one thing that I enjoy doing?

3] When was the last time I worked on a project that challenged me to grow? Who was involved in the project? What was my expectation before the project and after? What would I do differently if I did something similar?

4] What do I do during my breaks? Did I take a break today?

5] What is one thing I would change to improve my work productivity?

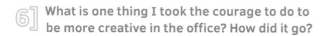

6 What is one thing I took the courage to do to be more creative in the office? How did it go?

Think like a detective. Every detail, no matter how small, will help you understand what intrigues you and how you can tie that into your work routine.

As a manager, it is important to create and foster a space and time for your teams to naturally be curious, open, and ask questions. How will you know what intrigues them if you barely know them?

Practice sincere intention and trust building. People know whether you are asking a question to get an open-ended response with their opinions or looking for the answer you want to hear. Having a team meeting where everyone agrees with you may sound harmonious, but this means no one is challenging you, thinking of new perspectives, or asking questions to dig deeper.

Before you criticize your team for not meeting your expectations, ask yourself about the possible causes. Are they rushed in meetings, overwhelmed at work, or are you really listening with an open mind? Most people are curious when they start a new job because they don't know the ways of the office or the daily routines. However, we are creators and creatures of habit and like to blend in. We learn how our colleagues present and take note so we present the same way. If we see in meetings that the manager isn't asking questions or listening to their peers' feedback why would we want to take the time to explore and ask questions? Therefore, as a manager, walking the talk in your actions, communication, and response is critical to team development. How you acknowledge a peer's idea, how you respond to a colleague's question, how you communicate your mistakes, and how you support your team members' new approaches gives your team the confidence and understanding that you support them.

Take a moment now to be honest with yourself. If someone is late with their deliverables how do you respond? Do you snap or do you ask them with curiosity what happened? That same question ("What happened?") with different intention and tone can imply different answers.

Again, before you ask for them to be more inquisitive and thoughtful, ask yourself how your own behavior is encouraging that space. For instance, when was the last time you had fun together as a team? In project development, how do you communicate the constraints so that everyone is more patient and understanding of one another? When facing a challenge from your managers, how do you communicate your own curiosity?

As a manager you are probably in numerous meetings back to back. I encourage you to find a way to break from the heavy meeting routines and find time to reflect and pause in the office. This will not only help you in your problem-solving process but inspire your team members to adopt this strategy.

Unfortunately, not everyone will have a leader who is supportive of their ideas and opinions. This realization can be disappointing especially when you start a new job, are assigned a new project, or join a new team. However, with a curious mindset we can take a proactive approach in how we handle these obstacles and still make time to protect our creativity.

For instance, what can you do if your manager keeps shutting down your ideas when he or she asked you to think of new ways to do something? This paradox can be frustrating at first but let's take a look with a curious eye.

First, pause and wonder why he or she is reacting that way and really listen to what they are saying. Is the manager saying these ideas are too expensive, complicated to execute, or vague? If the manager did not explain why, ask for an explanation and try to seek his or her understanding. They often have a reason why. Whether they think the idea is not possible or they think the timing is not ideal, it will be helpful for you to examine the situation from the manager's perspective. Second, seek to understand how your manager tends to make decisions and priorities. This may help you better understand why certain decisions are pushed back while others are immediately acted upon. Proactively observe and actively listen how he or she is communicating during meetings and in email. Third, determine when it's the right time to step up and step back. For example, is your manager sensitive about budget conversations at the end of the quarter? Have you noticed that your manager tends to delay decisions during the slower days of summer or during the winter holiday season? Understanding the timing and cycle of your office environment can help you strategize and know, with confidence, when it's time to push your ideas further and when to take a step back, observe, and let go.

The key in this practice is to stay grounded in wonder. If you are finding that uncovering these insights is hard instead of being disappointed, focus on why it feels hard to gather this information. If you are still feeling let down by your manager, even when you had long conversations, ask yourself why? Stay curious. By changing the way you think about the barriers, you can find new insights and new solutions.

In the meantime, continue to make time to be creative so that when you have those moments of discouragement you know how to cheer up and recharge.

As a company, this is a critical reminder to rethink about how you educate, empower, and support your employees. Take an honest look at your company. Where do your employees have the space to be curious, wonder, and ponder? What does it mean to have fun in the office? What questions do you want your employees to think more about? What are they having a hard time asking for or executing? How are you empowering your leadership to ask more questions and be curious as it relates to your leadership? As a company you have a bigger opportunity to foster both physical and cultural spaces for your employees to vuja de, which is seeing unfamiliar things in familiar places.

Investing in a creative physical space, educational program, and retreats is one way. However, I encourage the implementation of strategies that will embed this thinking in the daily routine. You have to truly show that your people feel that they have the permission to ask questions, and be curious. These strategies can be something as small as hanging up artwork or quotes or facilitating creative ice-breaking exercises during team meetings or department-wide meetings.

But how do you do that when everyone's interests and

needs are different: "We do not have a lot of resources or time to do fun stuff since we are busy!"

Understandable. The first question to work on if this is the case is defining what you mean by fun and work. Fun neither has to be exclusive, expensive, nor expansive. In fact, most employees start their job because they were genuinely interested in doing the work or knowing that they can learn something new. Once we remember this and take a new look at what it means to have fun it becomes easier to understand how might we tie fun and hard work to get both results: engaged employees and productivity. If you notice that your team and leadership need space to openly discuss and walk the talk, doing leadership team-building can be a powerful start. The key is to finding ways to create that culture and embed the understanding of acceptance to be curious and patient—that is where the power lies. In all, seeing things with a curious eye can help you find new ways to spark your employee and team's curiosity.

RECAP

While there are various tools, it is critical to first learn about your own learning preferences and root them in curiosity and discovery. Be an explorer not an observer and enjoy the journey. Ask questions and add time to wonder as you try to understand.

When we
are curious,
we ask questions,
we wonder,
we pause,

and we
ask again.

NOTES

7
A THOUSAND SHADES OF FAILURE

*"Think like a queen. A queen is not afraid to fail.
Failure is another stepping stone to greatness."*

—OPRAH WINFREY
Media Mogul, Actress, Producer, Philanthropist

What if you fail in the process of being creative? Of course we can't end our conversation on creativity without understanding failure and risk-taking. When doing something differently, there is always a risk and there are often consequences attached to that risk that we do not want to associate ourselves with. I used to have mixed feelings about this. It did not sit well with me that no matter how many inspirational stories I read of how others overcame failure, the fear of potentially being hurt, punished, or judged was huge.

Failure at work is even more daunting because it connects back to how others may perceive us and criticize us. And unlike other places, at work we continue to face them, work with them, and see them. Many clients I work with express how they would prefer to not try anything new out of fear of being judged, embarrassed, and looked down upon because they did something wrong.

It's understandable.

Why would you go out of your way to make a fool out of yourself? No matter how much leadership says on a poster that they will support mistakes and promote a good "fail-fast" environment, when they see their colleague's ideas being shut down, feedback being ignored, and their perspectives being judged, there is no positive motivation to share something new. There is little incentive to go out of our way and increase our chance of being judged.

The fear of failing is real and heavy. And it's a feeling we cannot ignore when we talk about creativity. I'm already feeling the negative energy weighing over me just by writing about failure. Experiencing fear isn't new. We've all experienced it one way or another—failed exams, broken hearts, lost jobs, betrayed friendships, failed projects, and unsuccessful businesses. The list goes on. But not all forms of failure leave us joking with our friends about that silly day a few years ago or encourage us to try again. Yes, having an open attitude to learn from mistakes is important but it does not always seem to work.

It's because failure is not black and white. Not all forms of failure are the same, yet we treat failure as if it only has one definition. Failure comes in a thousand shades.

Some experiences teach us how to do better, while others leave us feeling discouraged and hurt for a very long time. And some have the power to put us into shutdown mode.

Furthermore, life experience can cause us to become more cautious and less curious. We also learn to share less and to shy away from new things more. We also don't like to talk about failure much. Why go out of our way to talk about our bad sides when we want to show our good sides to others? Stanford Professor Tina Seelig articulates this well in her book *inGenius: A Crash Course on Creativity*.[9] Unlike children who are "naturally curious and intensely observant" while trying to figure out the world, as adults "we become skilled at predicting what we will experience and then we experience the thing we predict."

I do not think simply having "no fear" about fear is the solution since fear can be a helpful guide to reminding you where danger awaits. Fear reminds you to wear your seatbelt, to avoid jaywalking, to double check for typos before submitting that report, and to think again before you fire off that angry email. Our fear of losing someone teaches us how to value them.

So instead of being fearless, you'll want to make friends with courage and resilience. Like failure, courage comes in many shapes and sizes. You can have courage to speak up in a meeting, despite the fear of being criticized. You can have courage to support a colleague's good idea when your colleague is not there to advocate for him or herself. You can have courage to show up to a meeting with an open mind and pausing before responding with negative feedback. The more steps you take to be courageous the more you'll also learn to be resilient in facing new situations.

How you respond and understand failure matters more than the actual act of failure. Dr. Carol S. Dweck echoes this in her studies on fixed mindset and open mindset. In her book, *Mindset*, she illustrated the strikingly different ways students respond to receiving failing grades.[10] Those with a fixed mindset tended to be discouraged, avoided taking any effort to change, and blamed others for their ill fate. It led many to not only gradually do poorly but to also become depressed. Those with an open mindset, though upset about the feedback, worked harder, took more initiative to improve, took better care of their health, and accepted that their grades were due to their ill preparation. As a result, many not only significantly improved, but were happier by the end of the exams. Her research reminds us how we can find ourselves shutting down because we want things to be perfect. What if we start to look at failure as a catalyst for our growth?

Another aspect to note about failure is that setbacks come in various shapes and sizes. That is why certain things

may feel more daunting to us than they do to our colleague, or vice versa. Our worst nightmares are all slightly different because we all have built resilience and strengths toward different things. This is especially important to remember in a team setting for two reasons.

First, you can never undermine what others suffer or belittle their challenges. Instead, embrace them. Have an open conversation in order to better understand their comfort zone and their fear zone. This will help you find the best middle ground. Second, not everyone is going to respond to any given fear scenario the same way. For instance, when a sales quota is not met as a team, the entire sales team will get worried—but the root cause of that worry is different for each team member. For some, it may be the fear of not being able to feed their children if they lose their job. But for some, it may be a fear of disappointment, or feeling humiliated about the underperformance. You can see why a team leader's carrot and stick approach can be risky.

This also means that if a team has good collective insights and understanding of the real cause behind why each team member is afraid to fail, then they can overcome those moments better together, and transform with innovation. A team with a strong creative culture has a balanced understanding of fear and has a cushion to support one another's errors and mistakes. They also have a clear understanding of the absolute red lines that they cannot touch—allowing them to focus on pivoting and experimenting within their expanded comfort zones as a team. However, if the team is not well connected, then a team leader will have no idea why someone is upset or disgruntled and they will continue to remain apprehensive toward novelty, risk, and innovation.

How can your team feel supported when you keep hammering them to focus only on hitting profitability and targets, and ignore every other human aspect? If the response to failure is always negative, it is hard for our brains to see it as an opportunity.

There are two ways that you can encourage innovative mindsets, both as an individual and at work: a) build a reward system, and/or b) create a safe place where a certain degree of error is acceptable and encouraged. A reward system can be as simple as having an anonymous box celebrating risks employees took to be creative. The key is to find a way that connects the company's culture and work routine that will encourage people to feel excited to be recognized.

People need to know that, to a certain extent, making errors is okay. If they're not encouraged, they will naturally pivot around taking any risks. There are enough studies done on the subject that show that although humans are naturally wired to seek improvement, if the punishment for error is higher than the reward, it doesn't make sense and naturally they avoid it. Find a way that works for your organization, team, and your own routine where you can experiment, test, and try different angles and techniques. Monitor what works and what doesn't. Then do it again.

REFLECT

How are you doing? Ask yourself these questions as you reflect on failures and fear of creativity in the office:

* Why am I afraid of failing? What are things I stopped doing and started doing as a result of fear of failing?

* When was the last time I failed at something that I do not regret? Why? What was different?

* What is something that I used to fear that I no longer do? Why? What has changed? What is the same?

* Who are leaders you admire? Research their stories and learn how they overcame their failures and challenges by asking questions: What can I learn from them? What can I do today from what I learned from their journeys?

* As a manager, how can I make my team embrace risk-taking and be open to experimenting?

✳ As a manager, how will I know that my team is open to risk-taking and experimenting? If I do not know, what might I do to learn more?

✳ As a company, how might we foster a fail-fast company culture?

✳ As a company, what is the level of risk that is manageable? Do your people understand this?

✳ What other companies and leaders have successfully created a fail-fast culture? Which companies failed to do this? What can I learn from their successes and failures?

Remember, Thomas A. Edison tried more than 1,000 different ways to find the perfect light bulb. Stop complaining that it seems too risky or thinking that failure is bad. Study how other organizations and leaders have done it, and don't let that feeling of being inspired be the end of the process. Bring those insights back to your team and to your life. Say hello to various forms of failure and get comfortable with them!

APPLY

Let me be clear, you cannot live without failure. You cannot create something powerful without failing multiple times. The journey is supposed to be messy. Don't let that squiggly journey discourage you from continuing and moving forward. Learn to embrace your failures and take them with you as you build your courage and resilience. Just do it. Don't let your fear and need for perfection stop you. Dare to do more and dream more. Small and frequent practices are powerful ways to start.

Here are three things I recommend for individuals. First, practice embracing your fears and failures by being honest with yourself. What are your top five fears and why? What were your top five fears three years ago? How have they changed? When we start mapping out the different forms, sizes, and scales of fear, failing, and discouragement, the emotion becomes easier to manage, digest, and work with. You may also notice patterns to the type of fear you react more sensitively to and others that bother you less. These insights are critical to proactively preparing for how you will respond to failure. Also examine the patterns that emerge as you not only respond to the initial failure, but also how you heal from it and communicate about it. This is helpful information as you uncover and implement better solutions to coping with fear and failure—just like Thomas A. Edison.

> *"Many of life's failures are people who did not realize how close they were to success when they gave up."*

> *"I have not failed. I've just found 10,000 ways that won't work."*
> **—THOMAS A. EDISON**
> **Inventor**

Second, give yourself time to fully understand the current state of your comfort zone, and how it has evolved over time. Much of our fear is rooted in things we do not want to lose or are not comfortable doing. Consider documenting all the things you failed at and what you learned over time to understand also how your comfort zone continues to evolve. Take a look at things you feared three, seven, or ten years ago versus today.

Last, set aside intentional time to envision what future success will look like. Be as detailed as possible. What would it look like if you were able to overcome your fear and your suggestions were implemented by your company? What would it look like if your questions sparked a new policy change in the organization to better embrace diversity and inclusion? How would these help your work, your team, and your company?

We often spend so much time focusing on our fear and failures that we lose focus on the potential impact of our success. We become the very barrier to stopping ourselves from experiencing the joy of integrating creativity and reaching new levels of success.

Believing is only half of the journey so trust in yourself that you will get there, and you will.

Another strategy is to look back at your supervisors and peers. Who are the people that encouraged you to step out of your comfort zone, regardless of the possibility of failing? Who are the people who discouraged you to share or attempt anything new? Think about how you felt in each of these scenarios and how you can adjust your management style to inspire, not deter, your team members from innovating—without the fear of failure. Some of your team members may jump in with two feet. But others may need time to trust you and renew their own personal confidence so they can take a risk by being creative.

Let your people lead the exploration as you provide the map and serve as their guide.

As a company, how you communicate your failures—both externally and internally—will directly impact how your people respond to failure. Your response will reinforce your company's culture and values.

Another factor to consider, as you evaluate how your company responds to failure, are the inconsistencies that exist and how you honor, recognize, and promote them to your employees. Most people want to progress and improve, but these inconsistencies can make it difficult for them to understand how they can build a successful career in your company. Not setting clear boundaries or values on how you see failed work and effort also makes it easier for certain people or managers to discredit their team's effort too. This impacts the overall company culture and efforts to foster an open environment and failed experience space.

RECAP

There is no one single form of failure. Certain moments teach us more than the others. Everyone's greater fear is something different because we have all built up different levels of resilience. See how this all connects back to building a team that is more likely to embrace failure, yet still respects the organization's values, resources, and constraints.

Practice embracing your fears and failures

by being honest with yourself.

NOTES

CONCLUSION:
TRAPPED IN A BOX? THINK AGAIN.

"Do one thing every day that scares you."
—ELEANOR ROOSEVELT
Politician, Diplomat, Activist

When we talk about being stuck, stressed, and uninspired at work, I think we visualize ourselves being trapped in a box that is dark and cold. We feel isolated and helpless. That's why I think the phrase "thinking outside the box" became a term we've grown to love saying when we're referring to creativity. Because being outside is where we are not so limited or stuck.

Or is it?

If the box is dark, why don't we turn the lights on? Have we even explored what is already in the box? How are we so certain that there is no hidden universe inside the box that we have been searching for on the outside? We often see the box as a fixed and inflexible space. The truth is that as we learn, grow, and gain new professional and personal experiences, our perception of the world also evolves and changes with it. It's not the box that is fixed, it's our fixed perception that makes the box look immovable. If we look at it as a constantly moving thing, we will be able to see how the box also stretches and expands. This is why people with a strong creative mindset feel liberated and less stressed in the workplace—they know they can move and grow within their box as they wish.

Discounting the importance of having a comfort zone is also dangerous. For instance, let's look at your home. No matter what happens in your day, isn't it nice to have a comfortable home you can return to? I bet no one would like to come back to a home that looks different every day, nor would they appreciate having a night of uncomfortable sleep. Having a comfort zone, in fact, is important because you need time to pause, rest, and nourish your body and mind. Understanding your comfort zone is critical to being fully aware of where your unfamiliar territories and fear zones are, so you can venture out and test how far you can push each time you try it.

So yes, we may be in a box, but that box is not as fixed or small as we've made it seem. At the end of the day, after a wonderful adventure outside the box, we do like to come back home to our own comfortable box where we can rest and recharge. It's liberating to know that your worst enemy to creativity isn't being stuck but rather not trying and wanting to understand why you feel that way. Know that it is something you can truly work to get better at when you put in the right amount of effort, dedication, and persistence.

We have already spent so many decades wasting people's talents by undermining their true potential and creative value. We have already lost enough time letting the 87% of the global workforce feel unhappy and stuck at work. Isn't it about time we change this? There is, after all, so much opportunity to explore and grow together as we bring about this change together. Your courage to **be** creative and bring creative leadership to the table will inspire others to open up. In turn, they will encourage others to open up as well. Creativity is contagious, and creates a ripple effect. You can be the genesis of that ripple in your organization, community, and society. Some may call this a disruption, but I call this a movement.

Rethinking creativity has been the fuel to rediscovering what more I can do in life and ceasing to allow society's definition to limit my true potential. And I can't wait for you to experience the full effects of this powerful transformation.

Remember: we all exist within a box, but that box is a truly magical ever-growing universe that is powerful and limitless.

Give yourself the permission to let go.

YOU are limitless.

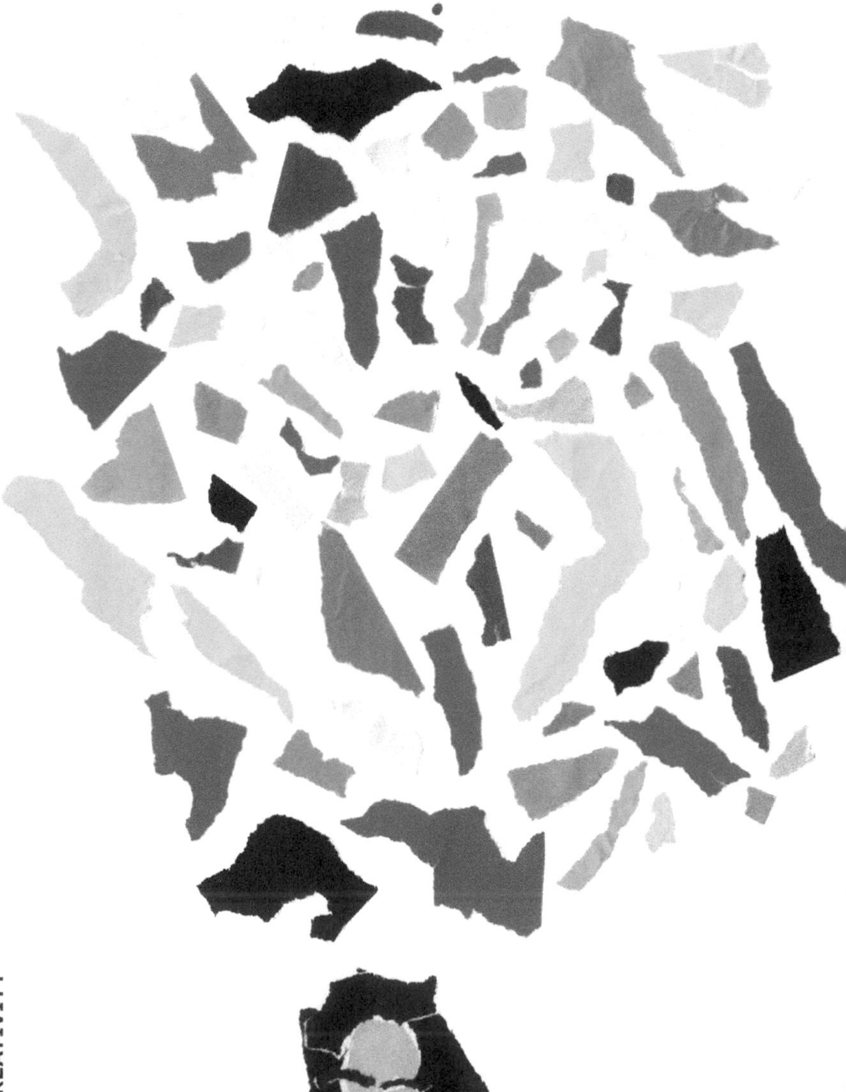

NOTES

AUTHOR'S THOUGHTS

Someone once told me how living as your true self can be both the easiest and the hardest thing in the world. I've thought about this throughout my life. While I've always loved reading, I feared writing and sharing my writings in public for a long time. Reading Anne Frank's diary in my childhood taught me how powerful your authentic voice can be when you put what you really think without pulling back on paper. I feared sharing my writing because I was not sure if I was good enough. I'm bad at hiding what I think or feel, so putting my thoughts into writing was putting myself in an open book and asking the world to accept the way I am.

What if people found out that I was not smart enough? Kind enough? I kept a diary for over twenty-five years where I practiced articulating my questions and thoughts, but still dreaded the possibility of someone opening them up and finding out that I was a fraud. How do I know what I know is right if I have yet to live more of my life? I wanted to write something worthy.

Writing this book and starting my company has been one of the many steps I took to use courage to face the fear I had of myself and to learn to better appreciate the journey of growing. Are there still people who will disagree with me? I'm sure there are. But that does not mean my experience and thoughts are false. Are there things that I'll want to improve in a few years as I learn more? There are—I am learning more each day. Is my fear of being judged naive or natural? It does not matter. What it took to be here and where else I will go because of these moments is what matters. And this is me speaking my truth.

I am who I am today because of the experiences and questions I asked. I am sure I will look back at this in a few years and will want to update how I express this message. But now I know that wanting to change is a good thing because that means I have grown since the last time I wrote this. This book has already gone through at least ten revisions during the two years I worked on it, and I'm excited to see how the book has evolved.

I am reflecting on these thoughts as I end my first book journey because I want to remember the adventure and lessons I learned.

One of these lessons is to go together if you want to go far. Writing a book on creativity to empower all has been a thought for a long while, but this journey would not be the same without the dedicated support of family, friends, and my publisher.

I want to express my deep gratitude to my parents who first taught me the importance of showing up with your 100% no matter what you do.

My journey would not be the same without Albert Kang, Aakriti Pandey, Jessica Collison, Michelle McGuire, Lindsay Young, Kristina Francis, and Monica Escobar—a few of those who reminded me each day why I should get this book and InnovatorsBox® out to the world.

Thank you, Jenn T. Grace and her team at Publish Your Purpose Press, who understood the potential of what this book could do by working with me to publish it. And thank you Heather B. Habelka for patiently helping me edit this book so that everyone can understand my message more easily.

Diamonds are not created overnight. I initially wanted to publish this book at the end of 2017. Things didn't go as planned. Thank God it did not. The book you have now is a richer and deeper version of what I want to communicate, and it would have been hasty of me to have rushed it. This day and age, we are used to getting things at our fingertips and I am guilty of that at times. I want to remember that if I want to create something of value, having persistent patience is key. Many invaluable things cannot be rushed. Enjoy the journey.

Last of all, the end of one chapter leads to a beginning of a new chapter. In addition to writing this book, I've longed to write books for young adults that take them on a new journey. Reading has been a powerful way to learn about value, perspective, and diversity. I want to help contribute to the next generation by leaving something that will help them question their routine in a new way and inspire them to seek resilience. As I was reaching the end of this book, I found myself spending hours daydreaming and writing drafts of my next book for young adults. The perfectionist part of my personality is now asking me to stop spilling more beans before I put higher expectations on myself that could create disappointment. So all I want to say is that I am excited to work on this new chapter of writing and share the results with you by 2020. But other than that, don't get too excited too early. I don't know what it will be either yet and I don't want to disappoint you.

Thank you all very much for taking the time to read this. I hope that this has inspired you and empowered you. Please share it and share your 100% with the world. If one more person can live up to their fullest potential with creativity, I know we will all benefit from it.

I look forward to hearing how you continue on your journey.

With love,

Monica Kang

September 2018

ADDITIONAL RESOURCES: YOU CAN NEVER STOP LEARNING.

"Creativity is contagious. Pass it on."
—ALBERT EINSTEIN
Physicist, Scientist

To complement your insightful journey to building a creative mindset, I wanted to share some of my go-to resources. They are listed in no particular order. If you have any suggestions to add to the resources, or if you have any questions, drop me a hello at monica@innovators box.com.

Thank yourself for taking the time to dive into your creativity.

I look forward to hearing your incredible stories of transformation.

BOOKS

For those who love reading books, find more book resources on our site at www.InnovatorsBox.com/books

Listed below are some of my favorites that I think you'll love:

* *A More Beautiful Question*—Warren Berger
* *Art of War*—Sun Tzu
* *Big Magic*—Elizabeth Gilbert
* *Creative Confidence*—Tom Kelley and David Kelley
* *Creativity, Inc.*—Ed Catmull
* *The Creative Habit*—Twyla Tharp
* *Flow*—Mihaly Csikszentmihalyi
* *inGenius* —Dr. Tina Seelig
* *Imagine*—Jonah Lehrer
* *The Little Prince*—Antoine de Saint-Exupery
* *Mindset*—Dr. Carol S. Dweck
* *Originals*—Adam Grant
* *The Power of Habit*—Charles Duhigg
* *Triumphs of Experience: The Men of the Harvard Grant Study*—George E. Vaillant
* *Wired to Create*—Dr. Scott Barry Kaufman and Carolyn Gregoire

KEY TOOLS

Here is a recap of the tools to use for your daily creative thinking activities and meeting prompts. Warning: Remember to add time to warm up at the beginning before jumping in immediately, and to end sessions with reflections to recap lessons learned. If you are doing creative thinking well, you may feel a bit tired—that's your creative thinking muscle at work!

5 Minutes of Daily Creativity

Consistency is key. Making time to do something different every day for five minutes can be a powerful way to practice thinking differently and pausing. Choose a time of day in the office when you can give yourself time to do something different.

How might I...

Asking questions is great. Asking open-ended questions is essential. If you are unsure where to start, try using the "How might I" question approach. This one often will help you stay open-minded since it does not lead you to forming a yes or no answer. This is why this term is often used in design thinking or innovation programing. You can push yourself and your team to think differently by posing more "How might I" questions in the work routine.

5 Whys

This is an iterative interrogative technique used to explore the underlying cause-and-effect relationships of a particular problem. The primary goal of the technique is to determine the root cause of a defect or problem by repeating the question "Why?" five times. This technique was formally developed by Taiichi Ohno and used within the Toyota Motor Corporation during the evolution of its manufacturing methodologies. This approach helped Toyota tackle malfunctioning errors and create a product consumers love. Understanding the root cause of a problem and solution can help you solve problems better in the future.

SCAMPER

A great tool to practice thinking differently in a structured way, **SCAMPER** was proposed by Alex Osborn in 1953 and was further developed by Bob Eberle in 1971. **SCAMPER** is an activity-based thinking process which can be performed by cooperative learning. First, define the topic you want to work on and the ideas and goals you had related to it. Then choose one of the options in **SCAMPER** to see how your ideas and thoughts change as a result of it. For instance:

* *Substitute* is coming up with another topic that is equivalent to the present topic

* *Combine* is adding information to the original topic

* *Adjust* is identifying ways to construct the topic

* _Modify_ is creatively changing the topic

* _Put to Other Uses_ is identifying possible scenarios and situations where this topic can be used

* _Eliminate_ is removing ideas or elements from the topic that are not valuable

* _Reverse and Rearrange_ is evolving a new concept from the original concept.

Forced Application

You can't force someone to be instantly creative but you can certainly use prompts to spark different thinking. Forced application is the process of using two unusual ideas, elements, or products and being forced to see what new ideas come from the relationship. This approach is a good way to practice thinking how everything has an opportunity to spark something new. For instance, If you have a black pen and an unopened chocolate bar, think of all the ways you can make a new product for elderly healthcare. Perhaps the chocolate inspires you to create something that is brown or chewy or comes in a bar shape. Perhaps the pen inspires you to document things or discover how to connect the two items in a unique way. Both objects can help inspire you to find new elements and think differently. The more random the objects are from one another the better.

InnovatorsBox® Games and Tools

My team and I have also created some card games and tools that you can easily use to spark creativity more easily in your collaboration, problem-solving, and decision making. Whether you are stuck in a brainstorming session, a team meeting, classrooms, a conversation with your date, or a family reunion with routine conversation, our products will come handy. Order your copy at www.InnovatorsBox.com/shop. Currently we have three series out.

SPARK is our signature creative card game series that empowers collaboration and communication. Learning how to think differently is important but can be hard if we have not done it in a while. SPARK question cards are divided into creativity, curiosity, and reflection to kindle your questioning and thinking, and to challenge you to think differently. It's great for brainstorming, networking, team building, and getting to know yourself better. You can pick from two versions. SPARK 1 is the green box and SPARK 2 is the yellow box. SPARK 1 is good to start with if you are exploring creative questioning with your team for the first time. SPARK 2 is good if you have completed SPARK 1 and want additional challenging and creative questions.

ReImagine is our motivation and inspiration series. Want to be more creative, but not sure how? No worries. Building a creative mindset is not an overnight transformation. It's a long and messy process, but it starts with taking small daily steps. You can have your dose of creative reminder either through the ReImagine notebooks or ReImagine cards, which is a deck of cards with 60 prompts to break your ordinary routine with creativity. Or have both to stay extra inspired.

Infinity series are games that help you with problem-solving and decision making. It takes time to change the way we think, process, and make decisions. To make that process easier, we created these prompts for you. Infinity Cards is a card game to use when you want to solve a problem in a different way and ensure you have asked all the different questions with your teams (or yourself). Infinity Squared is a dice game to practice asking different questions and formulating them. Both can be used to do problem-solving in a new way.

If you are interested in having my team at InnovatorsBox® guide creative thinking for your team in workshop, facilitation, speaking, or retreats, let me know. We'll be happy to spark your team's creative thinking!

ABOUT THE AUTHOR

MONICA H. KANG
Speaker. Educator. Author.

Monica H. Kang is an award-winning educator and internationally recognized speaker who is transforming today's workforce through the power of creativity. As the Founder and CEO of InnovatorsBox®, she is driven by the belief that everyone is innately creative, and that creativity can be used to catalyze personal and professional change.

Through her innovative workshops, consulting, products, and curriculum, Monica teaches creativity to Fortune 500 companies, higher education institutions, government entities, and nonprofits in a tangible, practical, and relatable way—regardless of industry or job title. Driven by her lifelong love of knowledge, she is an adjunct professor at BAU International University where she teaches entrepreneurship and leadership. Prior to InnovatorsBox®, Monica was a nuclear nonproliferation policy expert in international affairs. She holds an MA from SAIS Johns Hopkins University in Strategic Studies and International Economics and a BA from Boston University.

InnovatorsBox®

ABOUT INNOVATORSBOX®

InnovatorsBox® is a creative education firm that catalyzes sustainable change at the level where it matters the most: your mindset. We believe that everyone is innately creative, and that creativity has the power to solve every organization's challenges, no matter the industry. Whether you're addressing company culture, professional development, or any other organizational challenge, our customizable approach targets your specific pain point through creativity. Our educational programs, products, and interactive exercises help develop and grow professionals' creative mindsets to catalyze both personal and organizational change.

OUR PROGRAMS WORK

The benefits of InnovatorsBox® are not limited to a specific personal or organizational challenge because we target the root of every problem—the habits and mindsets of people. **In order to see fundamental changes at your organization, people need the opportunity to change the way they think through creativity.** As individuals incorporate creative thinking into their everyday lives, they'll be equipped to solve your organizational challenges now and any that may arise in the future.

Acknowledge the POSITIVE lessons learned from FAILED initiatives.

FOOTNOTES

1 Disclaimer: Depression is a medical illness that can be treated. Every individual can experience different symptoms and may need different kinds of support and treatment. I am not a certified health expert. My experience is one example of how depression affected me and how I overcame it. This is just my experience, which I hope can be helpful to others.

2 Dr. Seuss intentionally limited the number and length of words he used in order to provide children with fun stories that were easy to read and age appropriate. His publisher asked him to choose one- and two-syllable words from a list of 348. He used 236 of them for *The Cat in the Hat*, and it was a hit. Seuss's well-loved classics have sold more than 650 million copies worldwide. Source: https://www.thedailybeast.com/it-took-dr-seuss-a-year-to-write-the-cat-in-the-hatand-it-changed-kids-lit-forever

3 Sources: https://go.roberts.edu/leadingedge/the-great-choices-of-strategic-leaders and https://www.nytimes.com/2011/08/21/magazine/do-you-suffer-from-decision-fatigue.html?pagewanted=all&_r=0

4 This is one of the top classics to read when studying military strategy. Written during the Spring and Autumn period in China, each chapter is devoted to a distinct aspect of warfare and how that applies to military strategy and tactics. There are many lessons you can learn, even if you are not in the military because the book teaches you how to face "wars" without actually having to do battles. Many of these insights can used in business, education, sports, and politics.

5 Read more about Candy Chang's journey at https://candychang.com and https://www.ted.com/talks/candy_chang_before_i_die_i_want_to

6 For those interested in Sir Ken Robinson's work, I recommend reading and watching more of his talks where he breaks down how we can train more creative generations by changing things in the education system. If you can watch one TedTalk to better grasp the gaps and challenges in today's education learning system, my top recommendation is always going to be "Do schools kill creativity?" from 2014. The British author, speaker, and international advisor to education explains why today's formulaic education structure no longer works and is the cause of our next generation's talent gap. For instance, we are not in the Industry Revolution, and we know everyone is different. Yet we still set standards that expect everyone to follow one approach.

7 Warren Berger's study on questions was the first book that really challenged me to rethink the type of questions I ask and to not feel bad about asking more questions. This book shows deep insight into the research he has done in this field by interviewing a wide range of experts and individuals in order to study this human behavior. If you are interested in learning more about the power of beautiful questions, read this book.

8 The University of California, Davis conducted a series of experiments to discover what goes on in the brain when curiosity is aroused. Two key finding were that curiosity prepares the brain for learning and curiosity makes subsequent learning more rewarding. Not all curiosity is the same, but the consistent finding on this is fascinating. Read more about the findings at https://www.sciencedaily.com/releases/2011/10/111027150211.htm and https://www.edutopia.org/blog/why-curiosity-enhances-learning-marianne-stenger

9 For those who prefer learning by video, I recommend her talk at 99U from February 2014: "The 6 Characteristics of Truly Creative People." She shares powerful visual and sound examples of how environment makes an impact in our creative thinking.

10 I highly recommend this book to everyone. This helped me understand that no one is simply fixed or open-minded. We all have different things that we are more open to or not. However, understanding this helped me with how I saw my thinking process and the processes of others whom I agreed or disagreed with. If you are a manager, parent, or a leader, I strongly recommend this as your next reading. If you have a team that you struggle working with, read this as well.